DEDICATION

I dedicate this book to my husband Jenson. Thank you for being my biggest fan and supporter. Thank you for your patience and love. Thank you for growing alongside me and making my life feel like a constant surprise & adventure. To my daughters Bryanna & Kirsten, thank you for making me feel so incredibly loved. Thank you for letting me grow as a mother and a friend to you both. I am so proud of each of you for the unique stories of "you" that you each share with me. You have made my life a gift to enjoy with you both. To my granddaughter Avery June, you are the light of my life. I hope that the cycle of empowerment and love grows strong in you so that you may enjoy a life that is worthy of you and the happiness you have brought to our family. Thank you to my Mother for your strength, understanding and encouragement for me to share this book unedited and authentically. You are amazing. I'm sorry I didn't understand you until now. To my Daddy, I am so grateful to be your daughter and your friend. You are my hero. "Rock on." Thank you, Aunt Lela for always being a parachute to catch me when I was falling. To Emily Rose. Thank you for teaching me what unconditional love looks and feels like. And finally, to my Grandfather James Elmer Rhodes, thank you for being my Grandpa and the best friend a little girl could ever have. Last, to my "Tribe of Elephants." You are all my Dumbo feathers.

CONTENTS

FOREWORD

By Don Jose Ruiz

One of the most inspirational people I have met in my life is Franki. She has overcome the darkness in her life by opening her heart to witness her full potential. With her light and her love, she has rescued the "love of her life" which is herself.

Like a Phoenix, she has been resurrected in life, finding the strength in herself to overcome anything life throws at her. With that act of love being applied, she shares that love now with other people. People who are looking for love and light, looking to overcome their dark paths and leave their pasts behind them with healing and grow to the understanding that their perception of the darkness is not real anymore.

Franki teaches others to resurrect their life by using her teachings of The Five V's, which are the medicine that she used to heal herself and give her the strength to change her life. With full support of her beautiful heart she has now created a community of love and transformation all around her. Franki has made her way by helping the ones who have fallen into self-sabotage and the addiction to substances, knowing that there is an addiction which is much deeper than substances and self-sabotage. That is an addiction to suffering, and in that world, no one believes that they can overcome that way of life. But Franki is living proof that it can be done now.

She has this beautiful gift that she gives the world. Her words and her heart are laid out on the pages of this book. Sharing with others her own medicine of The Five V's to heal and resurrect the love of their lives. Teaching others to enjoy the rest of their lives in this beautiful world.

I am very honored to write this foreword for a woman that I respect and admire. A woman that I call my sister. We work for the same boss, and her story is a very powerful story. One that is what made her a woman of power that in my tradition we call a True Naguala (shaman, medicine woman). It is my joy to know that her teachings of The Five V's are now in your presence.

All my love, respect & gratitude…

Don Jose Ruiz
Author, Shaman

ACKNOWLEDGMENTS

I would like to acknowledge my mother Jessica for the long hours you spent looking this book over. You meticulously found every spelling & grammatical error and painstakingly corrected each one. Also, for adding insight to the content which gave me a better understanding of the full story. Your dedication to this piece of work was immense. I love you Mom. To Barbie Coder – thank you for your beautiful friendship and the GORGEOUS Book Cover you designed for me. OMG – wow! Also, thank you to Hayden Moser for being so patient and dedicated to helping me get this out to the world. To Alex Peterson for the amazing photographs you took. Finally, Jason & Teresa who graciously agreed to allow me to share "our story" together so these teachings could help others – thank you so very much. To Don Jose Ruiz who supported and encouraged me. I needed that, Mi Hermano. To all I may have forgotten in my excitement here - I love you all.

1

A NOTE FROM THE AUTHOR

"The very best thing you can do for the whole world is to make the most of yourself."
— **Wallace D. Wattles**

Hello.

You.

Beautiful soul.

Fellow teacher. Fellow Spiritual Warrior.

Fellow student. Fellow Nagual & Naguala.

Fellow human traveler. Fellow spiritual being.

I am so happy you have made it here to read this!

So- let me start by saying "Thank you."

Thank you for being open to share this adventure with me and explore the thoughts and experiences I have poured into this book. I'm excited to connect with the adventurer within yourself to explore some new ideas. New ideas which might challenge you and make you a little uncomfortable in the beginning.

As with any new teachings, I encourage you to read with an open mind and take what works for you. If it makes sense and you feel it could make your life easier, implement the ideas. If the ideas in this book are not for you, you may consider keeping them in mind for others you think may benefit from these teachings. I expect you will find something useful here, however. If not, that's okay too. I am sure that if you keep looking, you will find another book to be exactly what you are looking for. But for now, keep an open mind and read on.

It is my ultimate hope that you will find some part of this book helpful in healing your own heart. As a life coach and a teacher of the Law of Attraction, Empowerment, Recovery and Spirituality, it feels so good to have been able to create such a powerful and transforming set of teachings which have come to fruition from years of practice and learning. I have had the most amazing teachers myself.

I would also like to acknowledge the amazing teachers I have been able to learn and evolve from over the years.

Teachers in the form of other authors, speakers, students and personal acquaintances. My life is almost unrecognizable from where I began. I have definitely not become the woman I am today all by myself. It has been a long, winding, beautiful path to empowerment.

I have been blessed with having so many people who have encouraged me to write this book. Especially my students who have helped me learn and create this amazing process which I've come to call The Five V's. I am so grateful to you all.

Finally, I would like to say thank you again to my closest of teachers, my husband Jenson, my daughters Bryanna & Kirsten who have loved me through all of my evolutions, and my angel Emily Rose Olvera who taught me during her life to love Vulnerably and Unconditionally.

2

INTRODUCTION TO THE FIVE V'S

If you really think about it, any form of knowledge we have ever had the pleasure to learn has come from insight, imagination, experience or education of some form. Each person will have learned their own version of "The Truth" in their own unique experiences throughout their own life. After they learn these lessons and make a decision that "their version" of the truth is "The Truth", they start to consciously and unconsciously pass this knowledge to others. When passing on this knowledge, they sometimes impede on the right of others to choose their own truths. The life lessons of others can be extremely powerful in molding the world around them. The most powerful of teachings are those which are based in "The True Truth." I offer my version of all of the above in this chapter as well as throughout this book. I hope you enjoy it.

The Power of The True Truth

Back in 1997 I became aware that my life was not at all how I had envisioned it to be. On many levels, I found myself completely exhausted and lacking the belief that my life could be anything other than what I could see all around me at that time.

I was facing the end of yet another relationship and I found myself homeless with my two daughters, living in a homeless shelter surrounded by drugs and sadness. I looked in the mirror and felt empty. I barely had any fight left in me at that time. I was an alcoholic who was barely a few weeks sober. I literally thought all hope was lost.

I was surrounded by other people on the streets who felt the same as me and I began to settle into the inside dialogue in my mind that told me this was my life, and this was the way life was always going to be. I was convinced that no amount of self-help reading was EVER going to change the way things were. I had read the books by all the amazing authors I could find. Don Miguel Ruiz, Louise Hay, Wayne Dyer, Eckart Tolle, Florence Scovel Schinn... ad infinitum.

I read the words they wrote, and all I was left with was "well it must be nice to be them, but they haven't had my life... they obviously couldn't have the same self-talk as me." I thought to myself, "I must be the exception to the rule."

I remember 'trying' affirmations. I would tell myself "I am a loving child of light and deserve all the happiness in the world." "I am deserving of happiness." "My supply is endless, immediate and inexhaustible and comes to me under Grace in perfect ways." I would say these things with all the intentions of them being true and in a matter of minutes, I would be reminded by my own thoughts that I just simply COULD NOT or WOULD NOT be able to truly believe those words. EVER.

Luckily, I am a very stubborn person inside. Which allowed me to keep going even when all seemed lost.

I decided that if the affirmations failed to work in my life, it wouldn't be from lack of trying. So- I continued to repeat those words and many others throughout the day, not believing them and not really seeing any tangible results from them.

Ultimately, I felt frustration mixed with anger always creep up inside when I said these words. My head screamed louder and louder that I was fooling myself to think I could ever be anything more than what I thought of myself right then and there.

Boy, I couldn't have been any more correct. With thoughts like those about myself, I was lost before I even started. I had to find a way to keep in the positive but had no idea how. The books I read said to keep going, and I was determined to make the changes, so that's exactly what I did. I kept going.

As I look back now, the affirmations were working, albeit very slightly. But I couldn't see it from that vantage point.

What I hadn't really connected was the fact that after my "loving" affirmations, which I stated without much emotion or belief behind them, I continued my affirmations with super strong emotions stating the opposite. How could I resolve good thoughts when I immediately negated them with my negative and doomed "seemingly true inner thoughts."

I really wasn't yet aware that I had to pick and choose what thoughts I paid attention to. Those deep and destructive self-affirmation after-thoughts that were set so solidly in place at that moment were taking down any real progress I could have made by sabotaging me with negative words.

The things I thought were the Truth, were only my present truths. I had to get down to The True Truths.

This book will explore what I call the "True Truth" or "Vested Truths" from the experiences I've had by myself and with others. I will share them as I do in my live groups; as vulnerably as possible, so that the message and the beliefs behind the message, can be felt as clearly as possible. Some of the things you read in here may be a repeat of other things you have already learned, and that's ok. But the Five V's are my own teachings that I have uncovered and created through my Journey of self-discovery and empowerment.

Although I've been teaching the Five V's in live groups for many years now, I wanted to make a version of my teachings available so that my students can reference it at their own leisure.

It's a little bit funny. I have started writing this book over and over so many times that I can no longer count them. I originally began writing it after being asked again and again by a group of students, "When are you going to give me The Five V's in print?" "Where is my book?!" to which my response was always "Soon!" Or my infamous, "I'm about 3 weeks away from finishing it."

I would always begin, but I really didn't know how to finish putting everything I teach into words in a way that would cover everything I wanted to fully cover. I finally realized that any version of a book, as promised, was a good start. And so, here we are.

I fancy myself as a co-creator of new experiences with my students and clients. I say the word "fancy" because - well - I like the word. I am aware that some of my teachings may not connect with some people, and there may be critics who will find a reason to say that this "self-help stuff" doesn't really work. But I would rather face the critics humbly and honestly and say, "Hey - I'm just another human like you," - and also, "Yes, I've seen miracles happen in people's lives with just a few adjustments to their perceptions. This is simply something I can't keep to myself."

The years of process that I have experienced creating the 5 V's have been so incredibly freeing and heartfelt. The reactions and changes I have observed in my clients after teaching them the 5 Vs has been so overwhelmingly powerful, it has - on many occasions - brought me to tears.

How humbling it is to be able to help people heal from the grip of being a Victim to their own thinking patterns and land in a place of Vested Truth about who and what they truly are.

My hope is that this will happen for you as well.

At the end of this book I have included letters from my clients and students who have written some of their experiences regarding how their lives have changed since they have learned and implemented the Five Vs. They have given me permission to share their letters with you and I am so grateful that they have felt the power that the Five Vs has had in their lives to the point of sharing it with you. For now, I will be writing directly to you as to how you can put these Five Vs into practical application in your life. So- let's begin.

FRANKI OLINGER

3

SOME OF MY STORY

There are no greater obstacles in our lives than the ones we can see but do not understand; to ignore these obstacles and carry on as though they do not exist. In order to go where our hearts desire to go, we must first pinpoint our starting point.

Once we know and can admit where we truly are at, we can correctly map out a plan of action to go somewhere new, if we so desire. With this in mind, all sorts of new and wonderful experiences and adventures are possible.

Authenticity -noun

•The quality of being authentic.

Authentic -adjective

•made or done in the traditional or original way, or in a way that faithfully resembles an original

•Based on facts; accurate or reliable

•made or done in the traditional or original way, or in a way that faithfully resembles an original.

Oxford Dictionary

I AM FRANKI

My name is Franki Olinger. I am not a doctor, a psychologist, psychiatrist, therapist or any other kind of health or wellness professional you have ever known. I am an Empowerment, Life & Spiritual Coach. In the past, I have had some pretty traumatic things happen to me. I have suffered from addiction, self-sabotage, PTSD, depression, hopelessness, self-pity, self-loathing, etc… But worse than all of this, I have created ways of thinking and behaving which have left me unable to live a life without the addiction to the suffering I had experienced. In other words, I didn't know how to be happy when things were going bad – or good. But I found a way to recover which has been truly life changing. From the process of my own healing and helping others to heal as well, I have created The Five V's. I have used the Five V's in my professional and personal life as a way to get out of Victim thinking and into a Vested Mindset. This process has been created based on years of successful interaction and use between me and others.

I mainly do my work in person with clients, working

with students and groups during my workshops, retreats, speaking engagements or in one-on-one sessions. So-this book writing business is very new to me. I don't profess to be some profound author. Matter of fact, this is the very first book I have ever finished. You and I are experiencing a first with each other right now.

I am grateful to have been able to somehow put my thoughts on to paper and bring this dream to life.

I have been a Victim in many senses of the word. Rape, violence, abuse, lies, betrayal by those I trusted – you know, things other people would categorize as a Victim Situation. I also have been the victim of injustices, misunderstandings, confused opinions, fear, etc. You know, the things that are sometimes hard to categorize as "Victim Situations." In all of these moments, I have often found freedom through investigation and finding for myself, the "True Truth" about the value of my experiences. Sometimes the worst experiences bring the biggest self-awareness and lessons. I am so grateful for all of these moments, no matter how hard they were when I was in the middle of them. These life experiences have brought me to a new perspective and understanding of this life I am living. I truly am grateful to the

Universe for all of the gifts I have received in the form of people, pain, experiences, life lessons, struggles and adventures. These moments which have given birth to the need for me to have developed The Five V's. For the time I am on this earth, I hope to be a beacon of light for those I am called to help. I am simply but another human who has found some healing and felt called to share it with others.

I became an Empowerment Coach and a Teacher of the Universal Laws of Spirituality such as The Law of Attraction quite by accident. Along the way, I have developed a process in my coaching which I have named, "The 5 Vs."

The 5 Vs have proven to be very useful to others in healing limiting beliefs and misconceptions about themselves and others. This book is written with love and the intention of helping others find empowerment. If the teachings in this book resonate with you, then this book is for you. If they do not, I'm sure there is another book or teacher which will be more helpful to you. I hope you find all you are looking for here, though. From my heart to yours, I wish you an abundance of healing, love and The True Truth to be unveiled.

In time, I believe I will grow in knowledge and style. More insight will be revealed and thus, as I learn new processes, newer versions of this book will ultimately be published. But my message back to the Universe feels done right now, right here. I have been hesitant due to the nature of some of the content being personal or private or having legal issues to some or many. For this reason, I have changed names and locations to protect the privacy and anonymity of all.

So- rather than wait another three years to release it, as I have done more than once, I am setting it free. Are you ready to hear all this? Here goes!

Before I begin to tell you my story here, I want to make it clear to you that this book was written to help anyone who picked it up. No matter where you are in your personal evolution, this book will apply. Many of my clients are decades into their spiritual journey. Some of them are much farther along than I may be. Everyone has benefitted from the teachings I present here. For it is a new concept created from my own journey. It is offered to explore both new and old concepts in a unique and powerful way. So, if you are looking to expand your spiritual or personal "self-help" process, welcome. If this book is the very first book you are ever using to heal yourself, welcome. If either of you find that you are stuck in a cycle of thinking which has left you feeling trapped, I want you to know that as long as you are alive, anything can be changed and fixed. Any situation, no matter how scary, sad, devastating or painful it is, can be healed. So long as you are still here, your past can be re-framed, and your future can be changed with this book, a bit of perception adjustment and love. As long as you are still here on this journey as a human being, there is still hope. This hope and the creation of a new experience doesn't reside within anyone else; it can only be set in to motion for you - by you.

Even the book you are reading can be of help only if YOU are willing to take the actions suggested in this book. The decision lies solely in YOU.

If you don't want to change, if you are too addicted to your suffering, nothing can help. You must be **willing to allow yourself to be happy** in order for any happiness to manifest. In the beginning, this may seem harder than it sounds. If you are not there yet, don't worry, just keep reading.

Here is a little prayer I was taught years ago by a

trusted friend. I was struggling to be able to get past my own judgments owning certain new ideas and beliefs I desired to implement in my life. The prayer was called "The Set Aside Prayer."

You may want to try it for yourself if you so desire to open up to new ideas. It goes like this:

"Please let me set aside everything I think I know about this book, these words, my experiences, my truth, (insert any other blockage you may have), so I may have a new experience."

Now that we are both on the same page (pun intended) let me start with this: I have been blessed to have had many so-called "traumatic" experiences in my life. Those experiences have been observed from many different angles of perception. This book and the 5 Vs would not have been possible had I not gone through them.

The 5 Vs is a set of teachings I have created from my experiences over the past 40 or so years of my life. Again, some of the names and places have been altered so I may protect those who I believe have the right to anonymity.

I thank everyone for the roles they have played in my personal evolution. All of them have been blessings, no matter what the original thought of them during my experience has been.

You see, all of these people along the way were working with a mind that had been molded from their own childhood experiences. That makes their interaction with mine unique and a blessing that cannot be bought.

I believe this to be true. In the history of mankind, there has never be a child born with "issues." Each child is born with a clean slate, void of judgment, self-doubt, or hatred within. These things are learned behaviors - taught to us by our experiences, the people around us or our environments. As adults we can look at our personal situations with objectivity. A child cannot always comprehend or make sense of the pain or fear they are experiencing. When experiencing these moments, a child will perceive it with the child's mind, process it with the child's mind, and come to conclusions about the situation and their place in that situation with a child's mind as well.

As a child - thinking with my own limited understanding, with my own child's mind and with the depth of a child's understanding, some of the thoughts and perceptions I was so sure at the time were the Truth became hard planted in my mind as Facts. As I experienced pain and grief as a child, I gave each experience a meaning for myself and my value and held firmly onto those beliefs for dear life. I remember being confused or scared, and feeling insecure as I watched, experienced and tried to understand the things happening around me.

Thinking that I was somehow responsible for the problems which were happening around me, I created opinions based on my observations, or words that were said to me. Those opinions became MY Truth. These truths stayed solid as stone well into my adult life.

I created "false truths about myself" in my mind, which ruled my way of thinking. Until I began investigating those false truths and challenging them by asking myself questions about why these so-called truths were "The Truth", I could not see anything other than sadness for my future. Why was I still believing those things were still true today?

Why was I holding on to truths such as; "I am a burden." "I am unlovable." "I am selfish to want

FRANKI OLINGER

anything more for myself," or "I am unworthy of true happiness."

I could continue with so many more thoughts that always plagued me. But once I started asking myself "why" it was true, I started realizing that for many of these "Truths," I didn't really have a solid answer.

I started to question myself as if I was a child. I looked at the children around me and asked myself new questions like, "Was this child born unlovable or selfish or unworthy?" Is ANY child born these things? The answer was, simply, **"No."**

No child is born with any of these negative things. So- if the negative opinions of myself came from others, and I was not born with those thoughts, then how could I be sure that those opinions were actually "my Truth?" Most of my self-talk and self-worth had been adopted from other people's opinions or truths. That became clear and that was when my truths began to change.

As an adult, some of these truths have evolved through experience and growth to have different meaning than they had when I was younger. Like the thought that my mother was a bad mom. As a child, I was her toughest

25

critic. As an adult, I am her biggest fan.

My mother has lovingly agreed to allow me to tell parts of our story for the purpose of these teachings. My mother is an amazing and inspiring woman. That needs to be made clear so I can tell this story from my heart and without fear that someone may misjudge the characters of this story and the incredible parts that they played in helping me experience life as I have. I will forever be grateful to all of the humans who have played parts of Victim, Villain, Judge and Jury of my life. Had I not had these experiences exactly the way I had them, I may not have turned out to be the wonderful woman I am.

As a child, my mother used to talk to me about God. She taught me all about the Bible and the rules of God. I took it very much to heart. I remember feeling the deep importance of following God's rules. I aimed to be the most faithful little child of God I could be. God was VERY important to me. I learned that God loved his children. I also learned that God punished the sinners. I did not want to be a sinner, and I especially did not want to be punished.

I set out to please God in the best way I could, to show

him I was a "good girl" and was deserving of his love. At around 6 years old, I started to question whether or not I was doing something wrong. I was puzzled. Things just weren't right.

You see, I was being abused. For the purpose of this teaching, what exact abuse I was experiencing will remain undefined. I think you, the Reader, would do well to understand that ANY abuse a child feels they must keep to themselves in fear of the abuser being angry or of retaliation, is devastating. Whether it be verbal, physical, sexual, or psychological abuse. You as the Reader, can fill in the blanks with your own story, I am sure. It was abuse I kept to myself in fear of my abuser getting mad at me. I didn't feel like I was loved or protected from God anymore. I adopted a belief that I would never be able to be perfect enough for God to love me the way He loved other people. I believed that God was punishing my failure as a "good girl" by having someone abuse me. From the perspective of a child's mind, this was the most logical explanation I could come up with for the abuse to be justified.

I "knew" inside that even though I was following all of the rules, and doing what I was supposed to be doing, that God must see something inside of me worthy of punishment.

So- I adopted the belief that I was rotten inside and no matter how much I wanted to believe differently, there seemed to be every indication that this was true.

Can you imagine a little child believing they are bringing on abuse because they think there is something wrong with them inside, or that they simply aren't good enough? What a sad belief to adopt.

Today, I know that those thoughts are not true and never were true. God didn't hate me. I was unbelievably loved and trusted. Matter of fact, He trusted me with an incredibly powerful story and the ability to tell it to all who might benefit from these experiences. I was never unloved; I was gifted with a story!

A story of "Victim" which ended in a story of "Vested."

Today, I have a much better understanding of myself. I have been able to wiggle myself out of the Victim mentality which not only held me hostage to my old beliefs but doomed me to experience a perpetual cycle of being a Victim over and over again.

Over the years I have become very comfortable with saying the truth about myself. I frequently stand on stage as I introduce myself by saying, "My name is Franki and I 'was' a Professional Victim." I usually get some laughs from the audience or my students. I can laugh lightheartedly at the truth of these words, because those words no longer hold me hostage. Yes, those words are funny now, but they were not so funny at the time it was my Truth and my life was in shambles.

I can laugh about how good I was at playing the role of Victim now because for the past few decades I have been on a most incredible journey of self-discovery and recovery. I believe in the power of positive thought. I believe that I choose the direction of my destiny. I believe that nothing happens in this Divinely inspired world by mistake.

I teach the Law of Attraction, Spirituality, Empowerment & Self Love (among many other things). Knowing what I know now: That I attract what I most think about and that which I give the most amount of belief and emotional power to - I have made it my goal to embrace new thoughts and new beliefs which have become significantly more positive over the years.

That was not the case in the first 28 or so years of my life. I was angry. I felt like I had been robbed of this thing called "happiness" that seemed to come so easily to the rest of the world.

I have always had a VERY analytical mind. Even as a child, I was always wanting to understand the "Why's & How's" of everything in life. My head was concerned with figuring out the fundamentals of why I was being abused, molested, or punished. I was all too acutely aware that "God punishes sinners"... and all too acutely aware of the fact that I was told, "We are all sinners."

The fear of being punished is a tool many parents use to keep their children obedient and humble. My mother wanted me to get along in this world, and so she tried to harness my little ego and keep it small.   She accomplished this through my fear of punishment having already been programmed into my psyche that God punishes sinners and I was a sinner.

As a concept, I understand her reasons for all of this, after all - it was her job to domesticate me as a human and keep me safe.

As an adult woman today, I understand that my mother

was doing the best she could have done with the tools she had in life. As far as my mother went, I don't think that anyone is given the tools to deal with all that came along with being a young mother who was stuck in the life she was in. She was not happy like I thought she was. She had pain that she didn't share with me. As far as I could see, my mom was perfect in every way. I thought if anything was wrong, it was because I was the cause.

She had no way of knowing how I was perceiving and internalizing what she was trying to instill in me. She also was unaware that I was being abused by an adult male who was a family relation whom my mom trusted.

I was being abused and threatened by one adult and being told by another that "punishment" (which is what the abuse felt like) was handed out by God. I became convinced that God was punishing me with the abuse, and I was constantly trying to figure out why. What was I doing that merited this abuse? Here I was, being Victimized by this grown man, and somehow - I thought I must have caused it. I assumed I deserved it because I wasn't being enough of a "good girl."

To remedy my situation, I remember trying to do everything as perfectly as possible so that I would stop "bringing this on myself." That was a phrase this family relation would use quite often when he abused me, "You bring this on yourself."

From my earliest memories, this man had been abusive to me. He was a scary, selfish and violent man. He also had a taste for little girls.   I was, unfortunately, there and I was a little girl with no protection against him because I believed this was my punishment for being me. I had brought this upon myself. Besides, I couldn't figure it out. He was so devious.

I didn't know what he was doing when he was holding me down and tickling me, but my instincts told me that the way he pressed against me felt wrong. He would do it in front of everyone which bothered me the most. This "tickling" escalated to him coming into my bedroom during the daytime and eventually he started regularly showing up in the middle of the night when the rest of my family was sleeping.

I would lay there terrified as I pretended to be asleep, praying for him to get it over with as quickly as possible. Insomnia was a regular thing for me. I was afraid to go to sleep. I couldn't stay asleep. I felt unsafe in my own bedroom and carried this feeling everywhere when he was present. At the age of 12 years old, I finally told on him. Knowing what would happen, knowing I would be hurt if I told on him, I had kept my mouth shut for years.

One day my mother asked me on the way home from church; "Does he ever touch you?" I responded, "Every night."

There was a split moment of silence followed by the most wonderful words I had ever heard my mother say. She said something along the lines of "I promise, I will never let him touch you, ever again." What I heard was, "You are important, you matter, I love you and I am going to protect you now." All the years of "I'm not important, I'm invisible, I deserve whatever happens to me" felt like they were being erased.

I expected he would go to jail, the police would come, I would be safe.

No police arrested him, no jail happened, nothing happened to him. Instead, I was sent away to live with another family I had never met before. I would come to find out later in life that my mother had contacted the authorities and the family relation was forced to turn himself in and give a confession. She tells me that the authorities also spoke with me. The authorities told my mother that they had decided that pressing charges was not an option and my mother was forced to attend counseling and place me in a counseling program or she would be in trouble herself. I was so unhappy and afraid of this man coming around and so was she. So much so that she thought that letting me stay with a decent family, having my own room, new clothes and a chance at waking up each day in a good place would be best for me while she worked things out. But at the time, it felt personal. It felt like rejection. It felt like abandonment. It felt like betrayal.

As I settled into my new home, I thought a lot about why I had been sent there. I didn't understand - AT ALL. New thoughts came in droves of heated and wounded anger. I thought, "I must deserve this, "No one cares about me", "If I stick up for myself - I will be thrown away", "I'm worthless", "Not even my own mother wants me", etc. etc. etc.

I felt tossed aside, abandoned and betrayed. I grew increasingly more resentful. I made a decision. From here on out, NO ONE WOULD EVER GET CLOSE to me again. I WOULD NEVER TRUST ANYONE AGAIN! I would shut down and I would keep quiet.

I hated everyone who tried to say they cared, because I now knew that everyone really hated me, and no one really cared underneath their words and smiles. I also knew it was my fault and, sadly, I had grown to hate myself as well.

Worse than that, I now felt that I KNEW - FOR SURE- that I didn't matter to anyone, particularly my mother and especially "God."

I felt alone in my new home and every time my mother called to talk to me, I felt rage inside as I was called to come to the phone to speak with her. I held back my temper with each word that came out of my mouth. I wanted to tell her how much I hated her. I wanted to tell her how wrong she was about this man who, in my opinion, she chose to keep in her life while she threw me out. I wanted to tell her that **I MATTERED**! But I was convinced she didn't care, no one cared.

I devised plans of how to keep myself safe emotionally; lying to myself and rejecting others before they had the opportunity to reject me. I played the big shot and eventually became cruel and opinionated. All the while, I felt sickness and anger festering inside.

Thus, I had to find a way to stomach the guilt, shame, embarrassment, and everything else I felt inside. Nothing seemed to work. I prayed for an answer but the answer I received was not the answer I was looking for. The answer came in a very unexpected way.

I started High School in my new town. No one knew me there, so it was a bit easy to create a persona which made me feel safe. I decided I would put on this new "cool" persona. I changed my name from "Frannie" to "Franki" - a much cooler name for a tough girl and I shut the door on the little girl inside me as quickly as I could. I got good grades and did my best for the first few weeks of school, again, trying to control my feelings inside.

I would spend a lot of time by myself listening to music in my room. I put myself out there, tried out for the Pep Squad Dance Team and made it. This was at least something I could be happy with. I could dance in my room AND on the Dance Team and lose myself in the music. But- life took another drastic turn the night of my first homecoming dance at my new school.

No one asked me to go to this dance with them, but I was certainly not going to miss the chance to go a High School dance in my new town. I had never been allowed to go to a school dance before this because of my religion. We weren't allowed to go to outside functions of the "World". This was a new and exciting experience for me. Sadly, I never made it inside the actual dance, though.

I remember that night vividly. It was the mid 1980's so Pat Benatar was "in." I went and had my hair cut short exactly like hers. I tied that cool little bandana around my thigh as I wobbled forward in my "Candies" which were my first pair of high heel shoes and the very first mini skirt I had ever been allowed to wear. I felt guilty for wearing it, but God didn't seem to know that I existed anymore so he would get over it. This night, I was going to have fun!

As I walked across campus, I could feel the eyes of a few boys on me. Wondering to myself, "Do they think I'm cute?" I strutted forward, awkwardly, as one of the boys walked right up to me and knelt down and asked, "Are you sure you're at the right school?" Although I felt like I looked hot, I probably looked more like I was a 10-year-old boy in a mini skirt. Not sexy. Not voluptuous at all, and I guess I must have looked lost to him.

I answered him curtly, "No, I'm in the right place." He introduced himself as Jonas. I would soon find out that Jonas' girlfriend's best friend had witnessed our brief interaction and immediately ran to tell Jonas' girlfriend what she had seen.

About 5 minutes later, two hot-headed girls walked up and one of them pointed at me shouting, "That's her!" I had no idea what was going on until Torie walked up and attacked me. She shoved me so hard that I flew out of my little "Candies" high heels and landed solidly on the concrete behind me.

I heard the sound of a small tree branch breaking and looked down to see my elbow was bent and had moved two inches closer to my wrist. I realized that it wasn't my elbow but my forearm I was looking at. I was immediately sure my arm was broken. I looked up at her and in the most "matter of fact" voice said to her, "You broke my arm."

Torie looked back at me and screamed, "If you EVER

talk to my boyfriend again, I'll break your neck!" I was so confused by what she had done and said, but I had zero reaction. I figured it was just another fucked up thing that was God's way of punishing me. Maybe for the high heels? Maybe for the mini skirt? Or, maybe just because I was "me" and I had already established the fact that "He" hated "me."

I stood up and cradled my arm in my other arm as I walked to the front of the school and found a security guard. I showed him my arm and said, "I think my arm is broken." I didn't realize how bad it was until I saw his face.

I was quickly rushed to the hospital where my first experience with the magic of prescription pills was to be had.

The doctor acknowledged me with the kindest and calmest of manners as he explained to me that my arm would need to be "set". But, before this happened, he would need to "Give me something to make me feel better." To be honest, the pills did nothing to help with the pain of my broken arm. But I immediately felt a change in the way my thoughts felt to me. He proceeded to fix my arm which was, honestly, the most pain I had ever experienced before. He sent me home with those magic pills that would make my arm feel better.

Truth be told, even after I left the hospital, the pills still did nothing for my arm pain. But within the next few days I began to be acutely aware of the pain in my soul settling down.

I so clearly remember it- laying in my bed a few days after the broken arm incident and thinking to myself, "This is the best thing I have ever felt in my entire life. I don't feel any anger, any pain, no shame... I feel nothing! I need to feel this way for the rest of my life."

I was hooked. I got as many pills as I could get my hands on. Eventually the doctor would tell me, "I'm sorry, the cast has been off for weeks. I can't give you any more pain pills." So- I had to find an alternative. A new friend at school had the perfect replacement. She introduced me to Bacardi 151. It wasn't as easy to hide as pills were, but it seemed to be everywhere I went and easier to get.

Between the time I broke my arm and the time the cast came off, my whole outlook on life and school had changed. I went from obsessively trying to be perfect to not giving one single fuck about anything while I was high or drinking. Not giving a fuck soon landed me in detention for the first time ever and, rather than it being a "punishment," I viewed it as one of the single best things that could have ever happened in my life at that time.

Detention consisted of me, stuck in a room after school for 2 hours at a time, unable to talk to anyone around me.

I was allowed to bring two things into the room: 1. My books and homework. 2. A drink. It was the perfect storm. I would pour my alcohol into my Coke can, sit there and sip my drink and pretend to do my homework. I couldn't care less who was mad at me and I couldn't care less what anyone thought about me. I became rude and aloof to any authority figure who tried to connect with me. A byproduct of being dry and mouthy was that the other kids thought I was "so cool" as I laughed at teachers, threw textbooks at them when they tried to get me to behave and told them I couldn't care less about what they thought.

As I became more and more bitter towards the world, my foster family probably realized that they had bitten off more than they could chew. My grades dropped from being an A/B student on the Pep Squad Dance Team to not caring what my grades were. I am pretty sure, to everyone around me, it was apparent that I was on a downward spiral.

I returned to live with my mother and my family during that school year and, although I could have found healing in that return, I didn't. I was too far "inVested" in my numbness to let the drugs go. My internal pain needed servicing and I was too angry to face the family that I felt had discarded me.

From time to time, I sporadically encountered the man who abused me. Each time I saw him my mind would twist and turn violently. On one of those occasions, I remember him walking up behind me while I was outside standing by myself and he told me, "Now that I have you back, I'll never let anyone take you from me again."

I remember the sick feeling that sank into my gut from that interaction. I remember thinking that as long as I had drugs or alcohol, it wouldn't matter. I would be able to handle anything. That next year of my life is a complete blur to me. I mean, I remember maybe a few days out of that year, but that's it.

To be honest, I'm not too concerned about getting that time back. It's probably best I don't remember. I had drugs and alcohol and that's all that really mattered. For the next few years of my life, that was how I coped - if you call that coping. I ran away often and spent many nights out at different night clubs thanks to my trusty fake ID and some serious dancing skills. Everything felt completely insane.

I found myself at parties with men who were much more worldly and experienced than I was. It was both engaging and exciting to me to feel so much "older" than I was. It also, however landed me in some precarious situations. At this time, I had never been with a man. I thought it would be a beautiful experience when it finally happened, but my first experience was not the romantic situation I had daydreamed about in my mind.

I found myself one night in a bedroom with a man who was both charming and funny. We had started downstairs in the living room doing a bit of drugs and drinking when he singled me out and told me he had some cocaine in his bedroom upstairs and asked if I would go up to grab it with him. I thought nothing of it and followed him happily with a big smile on my face. He gestured to the guys downstairs and I was happy to be the subject of his manly "fist pump to the air" on the way up. I knew that I was a virgin and there was nothing to be fist pumping to his friends about, so I had no worries about going upstairs with him. As we reached his bedroom, he grabbed me with those strong arms of his and he kissed me. I felt so adult, so desirable to him as he threw me on his bed. We made out for a few minutes and his hand started to move lower on my body. I grabbed his hand and I smiled at him and told him, "I'm sorry, I can't." He replied with "sure you can." To which I giggled and said, "no- I can't." It became a little more aggressive from there and it ended up with me losing my virginity to a man laughing like it was a joke. He raped me. It was quick, it was painful. When he was done, he threw my bottoms at me and said, "See?! I told you you could." He then left me there by myself on the bed.

I was devastated and scared. I put my clothes on and quickly headed for the door. On my way down the stairs I heard him say "yep, another notch on my bedpost", as he laughed and high-fived his buddies. I ran downstairs and out the front door as I listened to them laughing as the door slammed.

You would think this would have curbed my enthusiasm for parties, but it didn't. I felt that I needed the attention, the drugs, the numb I so greatly craved. I avoided being alone with men from then on. But that would eventually change.

Time went by and no one got close, not one person got in, until I met "him." His name was Levi. I met him at a dance club. He was a couple of years older than me. He was "cool."

By this time, I was deep into my own private world of drug addiction and alcoholism. I still had the self-hatred and the feelings of being inadequate and worthless - but the numb that was brought on by the substances I put into my body made it all bearable. I was able to easily deny or at least cover up those uncomfortable feelings when they arose. I shaved my head and dyed my hair the most vivid colors I could find and made sure my eye makeup was as black as the night... I masterfully created the persona that I wanted others to see. I became the person I wanted others to see. I didn't care about "ANYTHING", nor did I need "ANYONE." That the mask I wore on the outside and that was what I told myself as well.

On the inside, and I mean deep inside, I was starving for someone to come along and tell me I was important. I ached for someone to acknowledge that I was smart, that I had talent, that I was worth their time. But I did not have any hope of that ever happening, so I drank and used pills. Of course, the more I drank and used pills to escape that empty place, the more I acted out and pushed away anyone who may have cared.

I felt and knew deep inside that I couldn't trust anyone, nor did anyone truly care about me. But when Levi came along, he said and did things that made me feel like I was important.

Of course, it wasn't exactly like that when I first met him. To be honest, he bothered me. I thought he was a showoff, so I tried my hardest to avoid him. But in his cute little ways, he eventually won me over.

I regularly competed in dance contests around Southern California because all of them gave out large cash prizes and that is how I partly funded my addiction and living on the streets on and off. Levi would always show up and compete against me in these dance contests. He really loved dancing as well, he never won any of our contests, but he gave it his all and I enjoyed that part about him. I had no idea how it was that every single dance contest I signed up for, he was there, smiling at me and signing up to compete against me. I found that odd.

I found out later on that he would call my friends to ask them where I would be that night and then he would show up. Los Angeles, Orange County, Riverside County, San Bernardino County - whichever County I was in, whatever dance club I was in, he was there. Trying to talk to me, trying to impress me. Flirting with all the girls, who all seemed to adore him. He was cute, but I wasn't buying it.

I finally started to give in to him after a night of partying at his brother's house. We had all gone back to hang out and drink after the club had shut down. I didn't know it was his brother's house until I came across a manila folder on the coffee table. Being the nosy person I was, I opened it up to see what was inside. I looked inside to find I was staring at these incredible drawings. One of them even looked like me.

Then, as I flipped through the drawings, I came

across my name. Over and over and over again, different drawn variations of my name "Franki" were there.

It wouldn't have even triggered my instincts if it wasn't for the particular way it was spelled. When I looked up at his brother, he laughed and said, "Not mine, my brother Levi's." Upon inquiring who his brother Levi was, the "dance club guy" magically appeared at the table with me. Levi sat down at the table and confessed that he had a total crush on me, and he thought I was pretty amazing.

I went home that night thinking about how much attention he had paid to me, and how much he seemed to really like me. He continued to show up everywhere I went. Later I would see graffiti paintings of my name all over town near the clubs we would go to that he had done trying to get my attention. In my "best mind" it made sense to me that "we should be together." Soon after that night was the beginning of my first love story. Or, was it the end of how I had imagined my "first love" story should look like?

I had zero self-esteem. I wanted so much for someone to "love me", "put me first" and, please, "make me feel like I am important." Levi did that for me.

Our relationship started out as a fun, playful and an excitement filled time. I was the center of his attention. He wouldn't let me out of his sight. He told me how much he loved me and how he would protect me. I felt overwhelmed but loved. As time went on, though, Levi became possessive and angered by the smallest things. It was kind of scary.

It wasn't long before I would come to find out that Levi was a troubled young man who was haunted by the memory of his father shooting himself in front of him and his brothers when he was a young boy. I am quite certain that he truly thought he loved me, but he was unpredictably jealous and controlling. He would constantly tell me how he wouldn't lose me. I was his.

Worse yet, at some times he was a cheater and a violent person. He scared me. I wanted to leave the relationship many times over the years, but I was so afraid and confused about whether or not I should actually do it.

The abuse became constant and he would say things to justify it like, "look what you make me do!" Or, "I love you so much I can't stand the thought of someone else having you, that's why I do this."

He would rape me, he would beat me, he would humiliate me, and I would stay because he would also tell me that everyone abandoned him and deep inside, I wanted to show him that someone would stay.

The longer I stayed, the more the abuse escalated. He would tell me that we were meant to be and that we should never abandon each other. I stayed because I thought it was what I deserved, and I also didn't want to be a bad person by abandoning him like he said he felt that his father and mother had done. I knew how it felt to be abandoned, and I resolved that I would never be someone who would abandon another human being who needed me.

As the years went by, our relationship got sicker. He would cheat on me and then make me become friends with the girls he cheated on me with. But if anyone so much as looked at me and I smiled back, I would get the "wrath of his love."

My drug addiction grew as I felt more need to numb myself. Levi would disappear for days or even weeks, and I was to stay home and wait for him. I knew he was with someone else during this time, but I was too afraid to leave my house, lest he stop by and make sure I was being a "good girlfriend" and waiting for him to return.

New Year's Eve 1987 I was at home alone that night. All of my friends tried to get me to come out with them. I hadn't seen Levi for almost 2 weeks. At that point, I needed to get out of the house. My friends talked me in to going to a local dance club with them. I loved dancing more than just about anything else, and so I went.

When I arrived there, I was told that many people had seen Levi with another girl for the past few weeks and asked me why we broke up. I was embarrassed, and also angry at the friends who said this to me. Levi told me that I should be wary of others who would try to break us up because they were jealous of our love, or they wanted to take me from him. I felt such opposing thoughts rushing around my head.

One of his friends in particular pulled me aside and told me he had been with Levi every night for the past few weeks and that he had another girlfriend now. It wasn't like this guy to lie, and so I sat there with my heart broken.

I signed up for the dance contest that night and I won. The prize was a large cash prize and I took that money and bought as much alcohol and drugs as I could get for it. I made a few new friends that night and stayed with them overnight. We partied throughout the night with plans to return to the nightclub the next night and do it all over again. I also got a New Year's Eve kiss from one of the boys in the group, which I admit I liked, but also felt very guilty about doing it.

I knew Levi was with another girl, but it still felt like cheating since he hadn't officially broken up with me.

We all went to the dance club late that next night. I think we showed up around 10 pm. As soon as I walked up, I got concerned looks from a few of my friends. They told me Levi had come looking for me and heard I was out the night before. They said he was angry with me and if I showed up, to stay there. My heart sank in my chest.

He showed up soon after with a smile on his face.

He told me about how he had met another girl and she was beautiful and funny and great. He also told me that he heard I had been there the night before.

I was afraid of him and carefully chose my words. I told him that I hadn't heard from him in days and that I was lonely and wanted to dance so I went out. Plus, it was New Year's Eve and he hadn't called or made plans with me. He asked me if I had heard him break up with me. I said, "no." He explained that if he hadn't broken up with me, then we weren't broken up. Then he started to try to hold me. I pulled away. He got that crazy look in his eyes and asked me if someone had turned me against him. I reassured him that no one had done that. He asked me if anyone kissed me for New Year's Eve and warned me not to lie to him. I knew if I didn't tell him, he would find out. I also knew that if I did tell him, I would put that guy in harm's way over an innocent kiss. I hesitated. He said, "Well, I will take that as a yes."

He started pointing to guys around us asking, "Is that him?! How about that one?!" When he finally landed on the right guy, I froze. The guy was across the street walking through the field on his way to go home. Levi ran after the guy and I followed him screaming for him to leave the poor guy alone.

A fight ensued and the guy explained that he wasn't interested in me, and he just wanted to go home. For some reason, Levi let him leave.

As he turned back around towards me, I saw the

anger in his eyes. He proceeded to punch me over and over again. He told me we were leaving and proceeded to walk with me over three miles back to his house.

The whole time we walked he was smacking me, punching me, spitting on me. He called me a whore, told me I was disgusting, shamed me for leading on someone else and trying to embarrass him. He repeatedly pushed me to the ground and stomped on me until my crying became too loud and he would pick me up and kick me and tell me to keep walking. By the time we arrived back to his house hours later, I was exhausted and bloody.

As we approached his house, he walked me over to the back wall. It was around 4am. He hit my head against the wall until I went unconscious. He then threw me over the 6-foot wall into his back yard. When I came to, I was inside a sleeping bag with the top tied shut. I heard him come out of his house and he walked over to the sleeping bag and kicked it over and over again. I thought I felt my ribs crack. I'm not sure if he had broken them or not, but it was very painful and difficult to breathe. Eventually he opened the sleeping bag and pulled me out of it.

He told me if I wanted to act like a whore, he would treat me like one. He raped me from behind. I've never felt pain or shame like that in my life. I cried and started to scream. He covered my mouth with his hands and told me in my ear, "I will fucking kill you if you wake my grandmother up!"

After he was finished, he told me he was going to go inside and make a ham sandwich and that I had better stay put. He was going to take a nap and would be back for me later.

I lay in that sleeping bag silent and too terrified to leave. I drifted in and out of consciousness. I woke to someone picking me up and saying, "He is gonna wake up soon, I'm taking you home." It was Levi's brother Jude. He carried me out to my car and drove me to my home. He carried my limp body up to my doorstep and rang the doorbell. My Dad opened the door and Jude handed me over to him. As I passed from Jude's arms to my Dad's, Jude said, "You have to get her away from my brother, he is going to kill her."

You would think that this would have been the end of that relationship. But Levi showed up after some time and begged me to forgive him. He told me that he wouldn't have reacted so badly if he didn't love me so much.

I was 17 at the time, and I didn't know what real love felt like. No one ever apologized to me for hurting me, I felt so confused. The more he talked, the more I was convinced that I needed to take him back, and that it was my fault for allowing another guy to kiss me on a holiday that I should have stayed home and waited for my boyfriend. I realized inside that this was all my fault and I needed to learn to behave.

Here is where the sickness really rears its ugly head. During this conversation, my Dad walked out on to the lawn and confronted Levi for what he had done to me. He told Levi that he was no longer welcome, and he wanted him to leave. Levi laughed and looked at me and said, "We are leaving now." My dad told him again that I wasn't going anywhere with him.

The words quickly turned into an altercation between the both of them in our front yard. My dad was only trying to protect me. Needless to say, my dad won. But I had already been turned. I yelled at my dad for hurting my boyfriend and I saw the grin Levi flashed as I got up and left with him. I feel such remorse for this moment, how

I screamed at my dad for doing such a thing. I was mean. I was unfair. My poor dad was left there expecting only the worst as I walked away with Levi and left.

The abuse subsided for a few weeks as Levi worked hard to create "a new improved man" for me. He dropped all the other girls on the side, and it was just going to be him and me from there on out. Of course, that didn't last.

Levi was involved in crime. His specialty was cars. He would steal cars and sell them and their parts for money. I had no idea what was really going on or how he was getting so much money. I didn't care though. He took me to Disneyland, dinner, dancing; everywhere he could think of to make me happy.

Eventually he became addicted to the rush of stealing the cars and couldn't keep it to himself. He would meet up with his friends with me in tow and he would hand me a gun. What the hell I was gonna do with a gun was beyond me! I was too afraid to say no though. He would make me stand by with the gun and "lookout" for anyone who may be coming. I stood there, shaking, as he would take a car and then yell at me to drive his car away and meet him in a designated spot.

I would love to try to say I was a car thief, but truthfully, I was just there with him. He became known as "the guy who could steal a car in 15 seconds or less." Everyone knew the time because he would bring a stopwatch and have people time him. Then he would stand there smiling as others recounted the time to him.

I didn't know any of these people or their names and I was happy to just be invisible with this particular crowd anyhow. I was just his silent girlfriend. He would smack me in front of them to show them his power with me. I would play the part for him. Too afraid to do anything other than that. Everyone watched silently as it happened. People were too afraid to talk to me about it because I would be the one who received the wrath of his anger for talking to another guy.

Only one person in that whole group of people ever came to my rescue. His name was Tyson. Tyson wasn't a fan of men hitting women. The first time he saw it done to me in front of him, he beat Levi up and told him that if he ever heard of him touching me again, he would find him and make sure he'd never be able to touch me again. Needless to say, Levi quickly changed his group of companions. It was the first time I'd ever seen him afraid of another person. It was also the beginning of when I started to see that maybe I didn't deserve what I was getting in this relationship.

I was safe for a while but, eventually, it started happening again. It was worse than ever. I allowed it because I assumed he had a lot of pent up rage he needed to let out. Sadly, the more I got beaten down, both mentally and physically, the less I cared about my own life.

Eventually, I became so depressed that I dove in to drinking and pills without reservation because, truly, moments of oblivion were my only solace. I knew eventually I would die by his hand; I just wasn't ready to go yet, so the drinking and pills kept me hanging on.

I started reading self-help books. Someone left me a copy of Jonathan Livingston Seagull and I read that book in one sitting. The words in that book changed something in my heart. I didn't quite know what had changed, but it was almost like I didn't feel so hopeless and alone anymore. Albeit a small little light at the end of a tunnel of hopelessness, I saw it.

I started to pray to God for the first time in a long time. I don't remember the prayers, but I remember the feeling of "please help me" behind the words. I read more books, and while I still got beaten, God was sending me little angels who whispered in my ear that I was worth more than what I was choosing for myself. No blame on anyone else, it was me choosing to stay. It was only me who could choose to leave.

In late 1988, 3 months after my 18th birthday, Levi showed up on my doorstep after being gone for a few weeks again. He had just gone to jail for grand theft auto and was out on his own recognizance. I didn't know he was out and as I pulled up to the front walkway of my house, I remember seeing him standing there and a cold feeling ran down my body. Fear. He was out of jail. Why was he there? What did he want?

I walked up the walkway towards my front door and he stepped forward to hug me. I remember being terrified as I backed away and I mustered up all the courage I had inside as I told him I didn't want to be with him anymore. I told him that he treated me poorly and I was tired of it.

I'll never forget the ice that ran through my veins as

he laughed at me and said, "I don't think you get this. You will always be my bitch and I will kill you before I let anyone else have you!" I knew he was capable of violence. I knew he had a temper. I knew someday either he would kill me or that something would have to come to a head with this. I was so scared. I had stayed with him many times before because of threats he had made towards my family should I decide to leave. There it was. He would kill me if I decided to leave.

I was stunned for a moment and pondered this option, realizing what my choices were: Stay and be continually abused or decide to leave and die.

My decision was almost instant. I was terrified but I said it out loud "Go ahead! Kill me! Put me out of my misery! I'd rather die than be with you!" He stared at me for a moment as he got a smile on his face and played the role of "calm and collected." He asked me to give him "one more chance."

I told him I was really done this time. I panicked inside as I tried to map out my escape route should he decide to come at me. But surprisingly, he didn't come after me. He told me that I would never leave him. I again repeated that we were done. Inside I knew that he had gotten the message. I spoke very carefully after this making sure not to ignite him.

He asked me to have sex with him "one last time." I figured it was easier to do it than to say no. He told me that if I did it, he would leave without an argument. I knew it was not like him to leave so quietly, but he did.

I ran into one of his friends in a nightclub years later. He saw me and told me that he needed to get something off of his chest. He recounted to me that on the night Levi died, Levi had gone to this friend's house and told him what had happened between us and that I had broken up with him. His friends weren't all nice people. This friend in particular had given him a gun and a ride back to my house a few hours later. The plan was that he would go in and kill me while the friend waited outside for him to return.

When they arrived later that night in the alley behind my house, I was in my room with about 7 of my friends in my bedroom with me. Half were there to party, the other half to be with me in case Levi came back to try and hurt me. A little after 11pm, my door flew open. There he was, Levi, standing there wide-eyed and crazed looking. He scanned the room and found me. I immediately stood up, afraid he would go after some of the guys in the room, and not knowing what to expect. He stepped forward - looked me in the eyes - pulled out a gun - said, "I love you Franki, I hope you're happy - here, watch this!" He put the gun to his head, looked me in the eyes and pulled the trigger.

I don't know if you'll ever have a moment to experience something like this (my hope is that you never do), but they say the eyes are the window to the soul. As the bullet entered his head, I saw his eyes go from insane, to shocked, to- I'm so sorry, to - absolutely nothing there. And then he fell out of the doorway of my bedroom and into the hall. I screamed and screamed. I jumped over his body and screamed. I felt a panic as I watched him dying there. He wasn't still like they show you in the movies. He was twitching and convulsing.

I saw the gun lying next to him and tried to wrap my mind around what the fuck had just happened. My head was screaming. In my head, he was dead because I broke up with him. I broke up with him and caused him to kill himself. The words in my head were cruel and vicious. I should have just let him beat me! I should have stayed! It's all my fault. I screamed out loud, over and over again until I tasted blood. When the ambulance showed up, the paramedics surrounded him and I was pulled away as I screamed at them, "Don't you let him die! Don't you let him fucking die!"

I spent that night at the hospital and across the street at Denny's. I was numb. I was in shock. I kept praying over and over again, "God, please don't let me become bitter."

Nightmares and PTSD followed. I couldn't eat. I couldn't sleep. I couldn't hear a car backfire or a door close loudly without dropping to the ground and covering my head. I was known as that fucked up chick whose boyfriend shot himself in front of her. For a time after that I lost touch with reality. I used to lay on the spot where his head landed and lose myself in the silence of that spot.

My mother and I disconnected from each other and although in the beginning I think she tried to help me; I was beyond any help she could have offered.

Our relationship came to a screeching halt over the whole incident. I was a broken soul. Unreachable. Empty and sad. Alone and devastated. Scared and confused. Judgmental of the God who had allowed all of this to happen in this way. I flip-flopped from anger and rage to suffocated panic to hopelessness and sadness, then finally- to emptiness. My self-esteem disappeared completely. I would spit at myself in mirrors. Scream at myself. I was so incredibly pissed at the hand of cards I had been dealt up until that time in my life that I could barely contain the rage at times. And God help you if you were a happy person around me because I hated you the most.

We buried Levi on a sunny day under a beautiful tree in the cemetery where his father was buried. I was drunk and on pills during the funeral. My lust for life disappeared alongside him in the ground where we left him.

I spent days on end walking nowhere. I don't remember this, but I've been told by others that I was like a walking zombie. Blank faced and empty.

I tried to go back to school to finish off my senior year, but I was unable to be present. The counselors at the school tried to help me, but I couldn't articulate anything to them. I didn't feel like talking about it. Every time I talked about it, I would start hysterically crying.

I remember my mother giving me a set of plates one time and telling me to throw them against the wall with all my might and break them. I thought to myself that she was crazy. I know now that she was trying to help me express my anger, but I wasn't able to reach those feelings yet. It was all buried. I was empty.

I left home shortly after that and lived on the streets. Sleeping where I could, even having a roll of cardboard behind a dumpster near the dance club where I would stay if I couldn't find a place to stay that night. Mostly I drank and took pills. People tried to help me. I could see the pity in their eyes but that only made me feel more anger.

I did not have the mental faculties to handle what was going on inside of me. Truthfully, it was probably better that I was so pent up about it. If I had let even an ounce of what was going on inside me out, it would've been a trip to the asylum for me. I had one outlet though.

One of the only things that I felt good doing was dancing. Believe it or not, in the 80's there were dance clubs on every corner. Or so it seemed. I could lose myself in the music and not have to talk to another human if I didn't want to. So, I danced and danced every night, literally for 5 hours straight without taking a break.

It felt good to just let the rhythm course through my body and let me feel something good. During the day when the dance clubs weren't open, I'd mostly sleep wherever I'd landed the night before. I spent almost 9 months on the streets this time.

I look back at the people who were there for me and it warms my heart to know that so many people were willing to take me in to sleep on their couches. I am not sure that if I met the person that I was back then, being the person I am today, I would've let me on my own couch. I was, at that time in full blown survival mode. I put on a face of strength and, "I don't give a fuck," when inside I felt so alone and afraid. I lashed out at people in anger. I manipulated drama, and I ruined friendships out of pure spite. I became a very sick and ugly person inside.

But somehow, I found people who felt sorry for me and tried so hard to help me. I wanted so badly for someone to love me, take me in and protect me. But I hurt almost every person who came near me once they started to get close. I wanted to die but didn't have the guts to kill myself. I prayed for God to help me again. After a bit of time I was eventually able to calm my head down enough to start to function and interact as a normal human being again. I rarely drew a sober breath during this time, however.

By the time I turned 19, I had spent a good amount of time on the streets. I had made many friends at the dance clubs that I went to. I had a friend who lived on a little farm in East Riverside whose family took me in for a few weeks. I saw her family and I felt a little pain inside my heart as I longed for the feeling of family, but felt I had none of my own.

One day, as we were sitting on her bed, her phone rang. She handed it to me, and I was surprised to hear my aunt's voice on the other end of the phone line. My aunt informed me that she had been looking for me for months and she was coming to get me and take me to live with her in Orange County. I hung up the phone for the first time in a long time with the feeling of being loved. As the phone hit the receiver, I broke down and sobbed with relief. I felt the nearness of Something greater than myself which was trying to heal my heart. I felt a little feeling of excitement in my heart as well at the thought of going back to Orange County. I was born in Orange County and I always knew that I would end up back there.

I was heartsick and grateful to finally be able to have a home again. When we got to her house, I felt for the first time in a few years like I could breathe. Like I could sleep safely. Like no one was gonna hurt me.

My aunt got me a job and helped me with some health issues I had developed due to not being able to take care of myself properly. I felt like an animal who was finally given a bath and gotten all the mange off. I got to drop the act of being this tough girl who wasn't affected by anything or anyone and just lay there and cry for a while. I felt her love so deeply. It was nice.

I convalesced at her home for a while before I returned to any kind of night life. When that time finally came, I felt like I was able to step outside and continue living again,

But like many other Victims, my circumstances had improved but I continued to think like a Victim, act like a Victim and create life from the point of being a Victim. Life moved forward. I continued to choose men who were abusive both physically and emotionally.

I've heard it said before that we will allow the same level of abuse in our relationships that we think we deserve. So, if I think I deserve to be beaten, I will allow someone to beat me. If I think I am not worthy of love, I will allow someone to treat me in an unloving way.

As far as my self-worth went, I didn't learn to respect my body, so being beaten and raped was something I didn't stop from happening, until I had finally had enough. Once I had decided that I didn't deserve that level of abuse from Levi, I broke it off with him. The next time I found myself in an abusive relationship, that guy was allowed less room to be physically and emotionally abusive to me, but once they crossed a certain line (even though I was understandably too scared to break it off with most of them) I would end it.

In my following relationships, a few things remained consistent. I always stayed too long; my "picker" seemed to be broken. I didn't seem to know how to be in a relationship unless there was some kind of sickness happening between myself and the other person. I didn't know how to function in a relationship with a person who treated me well. If they thought I was great, my head told me it was because they didn't know me well enough yet. I knew eventually they would see me for who I was, and they would start abusing me. I always knew in the back of my mind that it would eventually turn bad and so my guard never dropped. I ruined and sabotaged many relationships which could have been wonderful. I went from playing the Victim of others to becoming my very own Villain, robbing myself and anyone who might get close to me of experiencing anything deep enough to be real.

To say that my thinking was askew would be an understatement. I wanted to be loved unconditionally so badly that I created ridiculous ideas of things I should do to make my life better. Like, have a baby. I thought, if I had a baby… I would have someone there that would love me no matter what and would never leave me. Ugh.

Even writing that now makes me feel sad. Because I did bring a child in to this world to love. But being as damaged emotionally as I was, I was not fit at all to be pregnant or be a mother. I am so grateful that I went through with the pregnancy because the child who was created from that choice is truly amazing. But I wasn't there for that child. I left the father and gave the child to someone else to raise and protect. For reasons I won't go in to in this book, it was, in my mind, the best decision at the time. I felt that without me there, my child would be safer.

Looking back at this choice I had made; I have been able to gain a little bit of understanding for my mother who I believed had abandoned me. I wonder, was she really trying to protect me in her own way? Was she doing what I had done?

With every decision I made during my younger years, there was always a consequence. I didn't feel this then, but it is clear now. When I gave my child away, I felt shame and guilt. I felt like a failure. I was so afraid of being a bad mother that I chose not to be one at all. Even though, at the time, I believed it was the right thing to do, it did not feel good. I've never felt proud about this decision.

My insane thinking didn't stop there. I worked out a plan in my head that the next time I got into a relationship, I would find someone who had a kind heart and I would marry him as quickly as possible. I am still not sure what, about this plan, sounded like a good idea to me - but it did, and I found someone who was willing to marry me within 4 months of being together. A sweet guy who I had 2 more children with.

I played the part of "wife" quite well for a bit of time, but I was still not equipped to be in a relationship. I was walking through my life putting on an act. I was playing the role I thought would make me look and feel the most "together" all the time, still taking pills and drinking alcohol on top of it. As much as I would like to "believe" that I "wanted" life to be okay, I'm not sure that I honestly "did." How could that be truth? I mean, I didn't know how to be in a healthy relationship- and this guy I was with, this sweet guy with a kind heart obviously had a bad picker as well. After all, he had chosen me. I was the damaged goods he had chosen to marry and have children with. He married a pill popping alcoholic. It was par for the course. In feeling like I wasn't worth love, I always got myself into bad situations that I took on like they were normal.

He was kind and patient with me. And he stood by my side when I needed him to. But no matter how hard I tried; I could not reach that feeling of love for him that I wanted so badly to feel for him. In retrospect, I now know that I was not actually capable of falling in love with anyone yet. At the time, it brought a great sense of guilt to me.

Eventually, I ruined that relationship. It's interesting because we had two children. Beautiful daughters who were and are the lights of my life, but I still couldn't stop the self-destruction. I was failing as a mother, failing as a wife. What I had gone through with Levi had a pretty big effect on my emotional nature and it was like a festering sickness aching to explode out of my whole state of being.

I had, honestly, tried to live a totally normal life with that sweet man that I married, but it felt like, at every moment, I had to be my "best" to keep my sanity. Keeping all of my emotions under wraps was the best plan as far as I could see up until that point, but now, when I finally wanted to feel something, I couldn't. Eventually that relationship ended. Every time a relationship ended, I hated myself more.

The only thing I could feel was self-pity and self-loathing. I also loved the pity of others. I would tell them of all the problems I had survived, and they would show me pity. I was a great "Victim." Sometimes, I masked my wounds with false pride. The Pride that I had lived through my life up until that point and I was a "survivor." That's something that was always a "badge of honor" for me to wear.

The fact that I could go through so much bad stuff made me a survivor. I would tell people, "I am a survivor!" In the middle of my "surviving," it became necessary to have plenty of pills on hand. It always seemed to be better once I took a pill. Valium was my favorite. I called it Candy and I ate it like it was candy.

My Grandmother was my Candy Store. I feel so ashamed saying this now, but at the same time, I can't help but laugh at it. My Grandmother was actually one of my best suppliers. My grandmother had lost a leg when I was younger to heart disease and as she aged, I'm pretty sure there was either too much Valium in her system or she was becoming a bit senile. Either way, Grandma would always ask me on the phone how I was doing and if I wanted her to send me some of her candy that made her feel better. The first time I said yes, I was both shocked and hilariously surprised to receive a manila envelope FULL of Valium. There must have been 200 in that package. And from then on, whenever Grandma asked me if I wanted some candy, I was sure to say yes! Any manila envelope I saw in the mail was always quick to bring a smile to my face.

I drank and/or used pills almost every single day (aside from the times I was pregnant) from the time Levi died in 1988 until I got sober in 1997.

I remember looking at my two children right before I got sober and telling them that I felt sorry for them having to have me as a mother. They were both babies and didn't really understand what I was saying, but they seemed to understand that mommy was sad. They would hug me when I cried. For some reason, that both made me feel good and bad at the same time.

In 1997, I was a roaring tornado of a human being. I was not emotionally healthy, and I hadn't truly healed from anything that had happened even though I felt that I had come so far.

I had what is called a moment of clarity during the storm that was my life at the time.

Days before I had this moment of clarity, I had been let go of yet another job where my drinking had become escalated. I went home and I looked at my two daughters who I knew I was letting down and I sank into a deep depression. My recollection of all the happenings of this time is foggy due to the number of pills I was sneaking and the use of alcohol.

My mother had come to visit me at my home. It wasn't her fault that my head got louder about how much of a piece of shit I thought I was whenever she was around, but it did. I left home that night after she arrived, and I went on a bender for 3 days. I hid from my husband, I drank around the clock and by the time I was done, I was ready to get sober. I went home and announced that I was going to get sober. I topped it off with the announcement that I was leaving him. I could see the hurt in his eyes, but I didn't care. I was the bad guy, and so be it. When that relationship ended, it was the bottom I had so desperately wanted to avoid, but at the same time, I so desperately needed to experience. I had brought two innocent children into a world of chaos and emotional sickness. I wanted to blame God, I wanted to blame everyone for my sadness. But now, I had no one to blame but myself.

It was then that my healing truly began.

The lady who spurred me getting sober was named Marianne. I met Marianne in 1989, when I was a 19-

year-old kid. She was one of the classiest ladies I'd ever met. I was dating her son at the time. There was something about her that was magical. She seemed to see something in me worth loving. She could see me for who I was yet seemed to never make a judgment.

She recommended books for me to read, took me to groups and lectures dedicated to self-love and esteem building. She introduced me to the concept of "self-love." The most important thing she introduced me to was a little blue book that she referred to as the "Big Book." I remember reading the book and being so intrigued by the mastery by which it was written, especially by how much I identified with the words and stories. When I gave the book back to Marianne, I told her, "Wow, what a great book... too bad it doesn't apply to me."

 Marianne smiled and gently laughed as she said, "well - you let me know if you ever need this book back." I thought that was a weird thing to say about a book, but I smiled politely and agreed I would.

 It took until 1997 for me to understand what she meant and in January of that year I asked if I could have the book back.

I had become my own worst enemy and saw that I really needed to get in to a 12 Step Program and quit the drugs and the drinking. The day I gave Marianne the "Big Book" back was the last day I took a drug or a drink. I have to say, when I got sober, I still felt that God had it out for me. But there was a little spark of hope inside that said maybe, if I could become "good enough," if I quit drinking and I could find myself in grace, somehow, maybe the pain would stop.

I got to working the 12 steps of my recovery program as quickly as possible. If there was one thing I was good at, it was doing things over the top.

I healed rather slowly in the beginning. I had all of these people telling me how "worthy of love I was" and how "important I was to this 'Higher Power' who loved me" and all I could think was ... well, maybe He loves you - but I'm just here to get him to stop punishing me for whatever the hell I have done to Him that makes him hate me so much.

You see, I wasn't "fully convinced" yet that I was the problem. I blamed God, Levi, my Mother and whoever else I could think of. I was sure that all these terrible things that had happened to me was because God hated me.

I started speaking regularly in Speaker meetings and going to hospitals and institutions to tell my story. There aren't many stories like mine, so people were very inspired by it. I was happy to tell it so I could help people – but I still watched my every step so that I wouldn't anger my "Higher Power" in any way. I also played VERY SMALL in hopes that people would accept me.

I still often mistook pity for love as well. They sometimes felt similar.

I became a master at letting people feel like we were close, while still keeping them at an arm's distance. At the same time, I got really good at helping others to recover, which felt good, so I did that as much as I could.

My growth was exponential, but my bitterness towards life remained steadfast. I truly started to see God working in other people's lives, but still had this gnawing penchant for self-loathing which was eating me up inside.

They say that the phrase "Spiritual Awakening" is quite

literally a change in perception and I was well overdue for one of those. When it happened for me, it felt like the heavens had opened up, and it happened in the most unexpected way.

I was asked to speak one afternoon at a mental hospital in one of their treatment units. It was a locked-down facility which I had spoken at before in the adult unit- but what my friend failed to tell me was that today we would be speaking in an adolescent suicide ward where all the kids had tried to commit suicide within the past 7 days.

When I realized which ward we were in, I immediately felt panic rise up in my chest. "HOW DARE HE!" I thought. He knew that suicide was a huge part of my story. I can't talk to these kids about my experience. I was still mad. I was afraid I was going to say something wrong. It was just too close to my heart. It made me feel way too vulnerable.

I sat there as every kid introduced themselves one by one... except one. Leah. Leah refused to acknowledge we even existed. When it came to her, the staff said, "Don't worry about her she has refused to say anything since she got here."

I sat there in my chair and ran through escape plans in my mind; reasons why I could refuse to tell my story when my turn came. When it finally got to my turn, I started speaking, and it was the hardest time I've ever had opening my mouth. But I did it anyway. I told my story honestly and without holding back. I told it with love in my heart because I knew they were listening.

When we went to walk out of the hospital after the group was over, the most remarkable thing happened. I heard a little voice behind me say, "Franki."... As I turned around, there was Leah, standing there. She looked me in the eyes and said, "I think I could talk to you." So- I stayed for over an hour and talked to her.

During this interaction, I felt something shift in my heart. It became VERY apparent to me that I wasn't given this story because God hated me. I was given this story because He trusted me SO MUCH that He knew I would use this story to help and heal others.

I left the hospital, went to my car in the parking lot and sobbed for over 45 minutes straight, thanking my Higher Power for my story and for allowing me to have gone through what I went through. I finally saw "The True Truth" of my story. I have come to continue the process of applying the realization of "The True Truth" to every experience I've had, and it has freed me from so much suffering.

The years since have catapulted me into a life I would never had thought possible. I have morphed and journeyed and adventured into a life I can barely recognize anymore; one that is full of love, healing, light and joy.

I have played the role of and experienced all parts of the Five V's in my life:

- Victim
- Villain
- Visceral
- Vulnerable
- Vested

In finding the "True Truth" about each of my roles above, freedom has ensued and allowed me to create a path which has opened the door for so many others to find their "True Truths."

I travel all over the world speaking and creating inspiration and empowerment in others.

Along the years, I have come to see my seemingly

terrible experiences as amazing and powerful gifts in the classroom of life. A place in which I have learned to recognize what I have come to call the "True Truth." In following my heart, I have landed upon a wonderful understanding of the power behind tragedy and the danger in confusion. The Five Vs are a manifestation of following my heart and quite literally the process I have used to shift my life towards happiness. The Five V's have changed my life, as well as many others I have introduced the Five V's to.

I am so happy to offer them to you in hopes you can find healing too.

4

V1 - VICTIM

Consider this: If every child was born innocent and without opinions, judgment or prejudice - then in the beginning of our life, at birth - our slate was clean. As we learned to communicate with words and actions, we fell prey to abuse, confusion and separation. In essence, some part of our Vulnerability was Victimized. Therefore, Victim is not a "label" or a "bad word" but, rather, a "role" we have played. This "role" of "Victim" need not define us in the present.

Victim- Noun

• A person harmed, injured, or killed as a result of a crime, accident or other event or action.

• A person who is tricked or duped

Synonyms: sufferer, injured party, fool, loser, prey, fall guy, scapegoat, sacrifice

Oxford Dictionary

In my story I've been able to tell you about some pretty significant situations in my life where I have found myself in the position of being a Victim. But Victim isn't a "bad" word, but rather a role we have played in our story. It will only hold the meaning in which you choose to give it for yourself.

Before I was able to start my healing process, I had no desire to relieve myself of the label of "Victim" in any of my circumstances. Being a Victim allowed me to get around taking responsibility for anything that happened to me.

However, just the sound of that word brought on two totally different feelings inside of me.

On one hand, I felt like I was harmed and deserved to be comforted for the pain I had endured. On the other hand, the word "Victim" also brought about a feeling of disgust towards myself. I wanted people to know I was a Victim, but I really didn't want to be labeled as a Victim, if that makes sense.

I felt that if I were to be anything other than a Victim, it would mean I really was at fault, in some way, for all of the terrible things that had happened – or the choices I made which affected my life after the victimization. I had to stay the Victim to protect myself. In deciding to label myself a Victim, I could blame someone else for my brokenness. Being a Victim served me and my need to "not be the bad guy."

Before I was labeled a Victim, I had blamed myself for making God mad and bringing on the abuse of that man when I was a kid. I had blamed myself for so many years for breaking up with Levi and causing him to kill himself. I had scores of people affirm to me that none of those things had been my fault because I WAS THE VICTIM. For me to have admitted anything other than that I WAS THE VICTIM would have been very hard to do.

When I was finally able to look at my life from a healthy perspective, and admit the "True Truth" about everything, it was very freeing.

It was strangely comforting to me to understand that I was a Victim in all of these things. Although I didn't like the feeling I experienced while I played the role of a Victim, nor would I have chosen to go back and relive any of it, from my standpoint I didn't see that there were any other Victims in my scenario. There was a strange "pride" involved. I was the only person involved who was allowed to wear this label of "Victim." No one else could do that.

Fast forward to being an adult, having healed a bit, I realize now that when there is Victimization going on at ANY level, there are always more Victims than the main Victim.

For example, let's take a look at all the Victims in my story of being abused by that man:

Me: Obviously. Being a Victim of the abuse.

My mother: This family relation who had put me through all of the abuse had placed her in a situation that required her to make a choice which would alter the course of everyone's life, no matter what option she chose. She chose to give me away and place me with another family which caused me to hate her deep inside. Although I didn't understand it at the time, I understand it now. I would risk any of my children hating me and blaming me to get them out of harm's way. As a matter of fact, I found myself in the same situation as an adult with a child of my own a few years later.

My half-brother and half-sister: They paid the Victim

price of a broken family and the stress of a mother who was carrying around the feelings she carried surrounding it all. They didn't know what was happening with me. They only knew that their sister was no longer living in their home, and although they didn't understand it - they paid the Victim price of the discomfort it caused.

To this day, I am not terribly close with any of my siblings. Not from choice, but just because I wasn't there to bond with them. Absence and my choice to become an alcoholic and numb myself robbed them of a sister they could have gotten to know.

That's just a few of the Victims of that particular story. But there were many more.

There are what I call the "Extended Victims" of the story: Every person who wanted to connect with me that I just couldn't allow myself to feel safe enough to open up to. People who tried to love me who I straight up rejected. I'm talking about friends, lovers, neighbors, co-workers, even a stranger smiling in my direction on the street.

Most importantly: My children, who had a broken mother. A broken mother who didn't have a healthy grasp on Vulnerability and Unconditional Love to pass down to them. Each and every one of the people I have encountered in my life got a seemingly forever altered version of the original person I was born as.

This type of Victimization is quite common all over the world. Sometimes the Victimization is almost invisible. People pay indirectly for the damage done to others.

So- There is Direct Victimization and Indirect Victimization: For example, tyrants in our history have "directly victimized" whole generations of human beings. These tyrants have also "indirectly victimized" a whole generation of human beings who were born AFTER their reign of terror had ended.

There are families who will never be whole again or feel safe ever again because of these types of tyrants. Violence and death were produced by this type of human, as well as others who were under the influence of these people. Generation after generation of people will continue to pay the price of the oppressors that changed the course of their lives without ever even meeting them.

The learned behaviors of those Victims who came

before them will be passed down from one generation to the next. Being taught to "play small", "keep in line", "don't trust authorities", "just do what you're told and don't ask why" are just a few learned behaviors that are passed down from one generation to the next.

Even these tyrants have become this way because of what they were taught to be the truth. Let us not forget that these tyrants were victims of their own past experiences. None of them were born as tyrants. That is a learned trait passed down from one human to another. This is how the "clean slate" we are born with becomes filled with anger, fear and confusion.

Then there are those who aren't able to pinpoint a particular situation in which they feel they were Victimized in: Being a Victim doesn't require a huge and damaging situation to qualify. It can be just a simple word, or conversation which changes how we feel inside that does the trick.

When I was in the fourth grade I remember being on the playground and playing dodge ball. I loved dodge ball because I was pretty good at it. I was very tiny and could jump pretty high for my size, so it was exciting for me to be in the middle and it be so difficult for the other players to hit me. There was this one girl in my class by the name of Shelly. I thought Shelly was my friend.

One particular day, as hard as she tried, Shelly was unable to hit me with the ball. She got frustrated and I remember her yelling at me and telling me I was a slut. The other kids crowded around, laughed and pointed at me, and called me a slut with her. I had no idea what this word meant, but it sure felt bad and it stuck with me. I didn't know what to think about that!

I went home that day from school and asked my mother, "Mom what is a slut?" Her eyes got wide and she asked me where I heard that word. I told her that a girl in school called me one. My mother explained that a slut was a girl who messed around with a lot of boys and didn't respect her body. I remember being mortified that I would be called such a thing. Why had this girl thought I was a slut and why would she want to call me one?

It was one word. "Slut." Said one time. But from that moment on, I carried the fear that people really did see me as a slut. This really touched home because of my situation with my abuser. I took that horrible label very much to heart. My head made up stories for me in my mind about what people thought about me in school. I was SURE that everyone knew that she thought I was a slut. I changed the way I behaved on the playground and allowed myself to lose and get hit easier while we played dodge ball so that other people wouldn't think those things about me or call me names either.

One moment. One word.

It completely changed the way I acted on the playground for the rest of elementary school. That word also followed me through life. It wasn't a big deal as I look back on it now. And I'm pretty sure Shelly didn't really know what the word meant either. But it didn't need to be a big deal to alter the course of my life. That one four letter word was big enough to do just that.

In the dictionary, a Victim is defined as someone who is harmed, injured or killed as a result of a crime, accident, event or action. A Victim is also known as someone who loses out, is tricked or duped out of something they have a given right to receive, own or keep. In my experience, there are different levels of Victimization. Although some levels of Victimization may deliver more harm than others, all of them are equally important to acknowledge and understand. They ALL have the same power; the power to alter the way we view ourselves and this world, as well as the way we choose to show up and interact with the world around us.

I used to think there had to be a level of pain or violence from an outside source for someone to be called a Victim. Now I understand that, for many of us, there is a   much more subtle way we can become "Victim." Our innocence can fall Victim to fear. Fear, this word which seems to follow the entire world and everything we are sold, told and honed with.

Most news stories are offered with the premise of fear behind them. Many of the products we are sold use fear as their hook. To avoid being "ugly", "old", "fat", "unpopular", "out of style", etc. Then we are sold products to help us change how we feel so we are "good enough", "pretty enough", "smart enough", "valuable enough." Most sales pitches are offering a way out of feeling or appearing Vulnerable (I'll write more about this word later).

I believe every child is born Vulnerable, innocent and without limitations in their beliefs about life. Each time we encounter Victimization, it affects our opinions and the direction of our inner dialogue. It robs us of our Vulnerability. Worst of all, it creates this unnatural

"Visceral" feeling of fear. I have heard it said that there are only two things a child is born afraid of; loud noises and falling. After that, all the fears we have are developed or taught to us by the words, actions and/or inactions of others.

By now, you may have a feeling that I am trying to make you feel like you are a Victim; to turn the world into a place of Victims. That is not my intent. I do not want you to read this book and start walking around and looking at the places in your life where you are a Victim.

My hope is this: That we can discover exactly where the loss of innocence has happened in our own lives and get ourselves back to the pure "clean slate" of pure potential we were born with. The "clean slate" that through the years may have been snuffed out or quieted down. If you start to see that maybe some of your current beliefs may have been passed down or given to you by some person, place or situation which was not in your control, you are heading towards the "True Truth" about yourself.

Let's get one thing straight here and now. People who Victimize others are afraid. Apart from rare occurrences, I've observed fear to be the most common driving emotion of every person who Victimizes another human being. And Victimization comes in all shapes and sizes.

A child who wants to be held or comforted by a parent and then turned away is a Victim of her parent's inability to give them that hug. If a parent is too busy because they have to leave to go to work and are preoccupied with the fear of losing their home or not being able to feed their family, they may lash out at the child for "being needy", or "being selfish", or "being a burden."

This lashing out to an innocent child, in turn, can cause that child to experience fear, guilt, shame or even self-hatred and stop being Vulnerable enough to ask to be held or any other type of comfort.

Thus, the fear that the parent is experiencing causes them to lash out to the child, and the fear the child is experiencing causes them to recoil and stop interacting. As I said, fear is a most common driving emotion and here is an example of it being passed down to another generation.

During their formative years, a child is being

essentially domesticated by their parents in the art of what is acceptable and unacceptable. They are being taught to be proud of themselves or ashamed of themselves, and basically learning when they are officially considered a "good girl" or a "bad girl." They are being conditioned to embrace themselves or reject themselves.

These children become parents who become parents who pass down the family tradition of acceptable and unacceptable behavior to their offspring. They carry these rules of behavior into their everyday life. A child who becomes a parent can only pass down that which they know or have been taught through experience, conditioning or education.

A parent who wasn't taught how to be nurturing or affectionate may have a hard time knowing how to give those things to their own children. When asked for love or affection, they may feel inadequate or uncomfortable. So, not really knowing what to do, they may shame the child and say things like, "Stop crying," "Be a man," "Life isn't fair," "Grow up." Telling the child these things, in turn, can cause the child to stop asking for love or feel inadequate, and not worthy. The child will soon learn to consider these emotions as undesirable as they grow into adulthood and have their own children.

Because they never become comfortable with these emotions, they are likely to be unable to properly embrace and give these emotions to their own children. And so, the cycle continues on to the next generation.

A caregiver of a child who is short on money may say things like, "money doesn't grow on trees", "there are starving children in other countries", "stop being so selfish", "you should be happy with what you get", or my favorite; "people in hell want ice water"... Which just confused me to no end. Ha-ha. These sayings are obviously passed down from generation to generation and so are the emotions and feelings attached to them.

When we are very little, there is no fear or hesitation in asking for things we want or need, whether it's in an infant's cries, or a small child's words. As we grow older, we often learn to stop asking for what we want because we are punished or shamed for being a burden or needy of others. We learn to reject ourselves before someone else has a chance to reject us first.

Do you see the pattern? The reason I start with such

small things is to bring attention to the fact that some of our basic needs like "love", "affection", "food", "comfort", "safety", and "stability" are all among those things which are wanted by every child at the core of his or her existence.

When those basic wants or needs are not met with support, a child has a reaction. In the need to be accepted and loved by their parent, the child learns to rearrange their behavior along with their inner thoughts and feelings to align with whatever will bring the most acceptance by their parent. In my case, I learned not to ask for much.

From my own fear of rejection, I learned not to complain. From the fear of being shamed, I learned to pretend I was happy with things I was not happy with. I learned to pretend for fear of not being perceived as a "good girl" and the added fear being abused because of it. I learned to not open my mouth when I was being abused for fear of being sent away.

This is such a common theme that I hear from my students and clients. It became clear that people don't need to be beaten or molested to feel Victimized. And after a period of time most of them have a hard time allowing themselves to acknowledge that they had the right to want these basic human needs in the first place.

Whether you have had traumatic experiences or not, most people have been Victimized by intentional or unintentional conditioning to some degree.

Whenever you become Vulnerable and are damaged in some way as a result of expressing your Vulnerability, that is also what we could call a Victim Situation in this book. If you are confused about whether or not your experience can be called a "Victimization," let's put it simply:

A "Victim Situation" is one that changes or alters either our path, our behavior, our thinking, or our feelings about ourselves, life, other people, our reality, or this world. A "Victim Situation" causes us to reject our own Truth. A "Victim Situation" causes us to rob ourselves of the things every human deserves, like happiness, security, joy, love, etc.

Being a Victim alters our emotions, choices and lives. This alteration leads us further away from our **"authentic self"** and into **"unhealthy delusion."** Unhealthy delusion is the story that we tell ourselves to feel better about what we allow to have happen in our life. This delusion is birthed by what I have come to know as **"limiting beliefs."**

The beliefs which serve us and support our "greater good" are called "empowering beliefs." The ones which limit, confuse and suffocate our dreams and aspirations are our "limiting beliefs."

We are all born with full potential. As we are molded by the beliefs and rules of our parents, society and all of those who influence us while we are growing up, we learn what we **should** believe we are worth, what we **should** believe we are capable of and what we **should** believe we deserve. We hold these beliefs in our core and we continuously access these beliefs as we go through our lives and make decisions about our present and future circumstances.

As we grow into adulthood, our original unlimited potential will have been molded into a very precise belief system which tells us what we are (and are not) allowed to want, or even need.

The truth is this: If I were ask you to imagine every infant in the world, lined up in a row, and then ask you to point out and choose the babies who don't deserve to be fed, held, comforted, loved, be successful, be happy, be provided for, and so on... I can almost GUARANTEE you would not identify any of these small beings to be undeserving of any of the above things.

As a matter of fact, there would probably be no judgment of any child, at all, until the parents walked into the room and stood next to the children; then there may be some judgments. But the "True Truth" is; every baby deserves all the happiness, nurturing, love and security in the world. Every baby is born filled with enormous potential. Every baby is born with the natural, everyday desires of wanting to be loved, nourished, and cared for. No child is born with shame, guilt and/or self-hatred. That is learned later on.

So, when a child is told either by words or actions that they do not deserve these things, or the child is told they are doing something wrong by wanting these things – that is when I see the child as being Victimized. The parents are not trying nor are they intending to Victimize the child, but their behavior toward the child results in that child's natural security and desires being diminished.

If any part of you is feeling uneasy inside, there is a chance you've had some experience with this, either as the parent OR the child.

In my opinion, a good friend of mine said it perfectly, "If your parents left you standing in the rain as a child, shame on them... but if you are still standing in the rain as an adult blaming your parents, shame on you." (sorry to say the shame word, but you get what I'm saying).

My hope is not that you will take the road of dissecting whether my words are correct or not, but to simply acknowledge that you recognize these facts:

- *All humans deserve to be happy, loved, comforted, and complete.*
- *All humans deserve to know and feel that they are valuable and have unique worth as individuals.*
- *All false, limiting beliefs are from direct teaching or experiential learning situations.*

When our wants and needs were pushed aside as children, we started adopting newfound beliefs that told us we were wrong for being "needy." Our adopting of these beliefs about ourselves were quite often "not optional" for many of us. We either adopted these beliefs or we felt the pain of punishment, rejection or shame for not doing so.

Great news! These limiting beliefs are also ones that can be healed. But first we must have a little more introspection.

One of the hardest things about getting past the first "V" is being able to say those words. "I was Victimized." Many people don't like the way it sounds, feels or defines them. Many people still have the messages they internalized as children clouding their thoughts and cannot even use the word "Victim" without it sparking anger or disdain towards the idea of it being true for themselves. Some people find it ludicrous that they could claim they were a Victim at all. Some believe their childhood was perfect and without any discomfort.

Take it easy on yourself. I'm not asking you to say you had bad parents. I'm asking you to just connect to the possibility that you may have encountered and misunderstood a parent, a teacher or another adult' s intentions when you were little. Or maybe your parents were not equipped by their parents or their culture didn't allow them to give you everything you emotionally needed or required. And, for those of you like me, who know exactly how you were Victimized, either verbally, physically, sexually, or psychologically, I am giving you a clear moment and total permission to say this out loud, **"I, DESERVED BETTER THAN WHAT I GOT!"**

I have found that owning the fact that I was a "Victim" hasn't hindered my growth one bit. On the contrary, it has given me a place to grow from. It is a starting point. A place I can begin from, but do not wish to remain in. One of the most important things we can do when we are lost is pull over and ask for directions. In order to leave that place (being lost), we have to know where we are coming from, and then proceed with how to get out of there. I don't necessarily like the sound of the words "I am a Victim" coming out of my mouth, but I believe in the phrase, "The truth shall set you free." In owning that saying and finding my Truth about being a "Victim," I have taken my power back and I can now grow in a whole new direction.

Once you can embrace this small truth, I recommend you start finding a way out. Do not sit too long in the Victim role, for it is a quicksand to the soul.

It is freeing, healing, even necessary to recognize when you are in the Victim role in order to get out of Victimville. Victimville is a confusing place to be. Sometimes it may be masked as something else. Some may not even know they are there. Some may reject the word Victim altogether and remain lost and confused forever.

When we reject the ability to acknowledge the Victim role, we have already begun to identify and act in line with the next "V."

VILLAIN.

When we reject growth, or close our minds to new concepts or ideas that seem scary or foreign, we are placing ourselves in a position of "trapped." We are in a sense Victimizing ourselves and creating a perpetual cycle of confusion, frustration and becoming our own Villain.

I know that for me, I have a choice. Am I a Victim to others actions and behaviors? Sometimes, the answer is YES. Which brings me to the next choice I face. Am I going to allow myself to stay in the Victim role? If I choose to accept and remain in the Victim role, I am doomed to experience a life full of suffering. In this role, I have chosen to give all of my personal power to the Villain. If I refuse to find my way out of the victim role, I too – am the Villain. My own villain.

When working with my clients and students during this process, I have experienced many forms of Victim mindsets. I have walked through my client's personal experiences of being the Victim with them on so many different levels. My clients & students have all had Victim/Villain experiences which has left them to suffer with crippling bouts of PTSD, depression, anger, paralyzing fear, homelessness, financial despair, lost relationships, self-hatred, addiction, confusion, etc. The list could fill this entire book. But the one thing that has remained true in every single one of these cases is this; Once they can admit that they were in the role of Victim (either to others or themselves), they have all found a way to move forward and find freedom from the bondage of these experiences or the thoughts surrounding them.

In working on the Victim part of the Five V's, I usually start with having the client imagine themselves as an innocent newborn. The day they were born, they experienced pure love and pure potential for their lives.

There in the beginning is that moments mind-state that we can acknowledge as the perfect mind-state. From that moment on, we became inundated with outside opinions and stimulation. The more we began to learn "should and shouldn'ts", the more we lost our "could's and would's". Our pure potential diminished as we were trained to think and act like the others around us. The potential we were born with was slowly erased and replaced with rules and boundaries. Not every rule and boundary was harmful. Most were for our safety. But somewhere along the line, some of us forgot who we could be and were convinced rather of what we should be, or who we could never be.

Well, let me stop you right there. If any part of you is trying not to identify with the victim role, let me ask you this. Do you think you are experiencing life in its full potential? If the answer is yes, I love it! Please throw this book away and write one for me to read. The world needs your wisdom!

But if you are not experiencing life in its full potential, ask yourself why you are living the way you are. What little voice inside is holding you hostage to someone else's rules and beliefs? Even better, what circumstance in your life are you being held hostage in? Could you leave? If you can't leave, why? Even if you are sitting on death row in prison, you are only trapped by your state of mind. Are you a Victim? Or a Villain? If you WERE a Victim or a Villain, why are you still feeling that in the present?

No matter who you were yesterday, or even 10 minutes ago – that is not who you have to be permanently. You can choose at any time to return to the person you were born as and make new choices which serve the world with a better version of you. Start the process today of forgiving yourself for not being your authentic self and give yourself the gift of self-love, even if it's for those around you to benefit from.

If you are stuck in an abusive relationship, get out.

If you hate your job, find a new one.

If you are stuck in a cycle of addiction, challenge yourself to make new choices (even if it's one minute at a time.)

If you are choosing ANYTHING less than you would choose for a newborn baby's future plan, you are robbing yourself of what you are capable of.

Stop being the Victim of others or yourself.

Sometimes I will have my clients go through their lives from birth up to the present and make a list of EVERY time they were a Victim. Every time their feelings were hurt. Every time a dream was shut down. I have them list EVERY SINGLE INCIDENT THAT COMES TO MIND and we will go through them one by one and ask ourselves where the LIE sits.

Yes, being a Victim means that you are believing a lie about yourself, the world or life. A lie about these things, coupled with self-definition using these lies will trap you forever in a cycle of Victim / Villain until you return to The True Truth.

We state the True Truths alongside every Victim situation they write down. For most people, it is a freeing process. For some that feel even more trapped after doing this process, we can usually rectify it with the rest of the work. I've yet to see someone do this process and not have a profound shift in their life.

Freedom comes through The True Truth. Everyone was born with a Divine Right to flourish and experience adventure, joy, abundance and happiness. Those in a Victim mindset will allow for those things to be taken away indefinitely.

I know that you may have to take a moment to digest some of the things I have written in this chapter. Take all the time you need. But if you are in the slightest way open to gaining some new perspective on life, continue with an open mind.

Viktor Frankl, in his book Man's Search for Meaning wrote, "When we are no longer able to change a situation, we are challenged to change ourselves," which to me, has multiple meanings. He was, of course, writing about his own situation while enslaved in a concentration camp. But what of the past? What about the situations we can no longer go back in time and rearrange? Where do we go from there?

Let's next look at the opposite side of Victim thinking. The role of the Villain.

New Thoughts About Being A "Victim"

- Do you now understand that Victim is NOT necessarily a "bad" word?
- Where were you 'Victimized' as a child?
- What were the circumstances?
- What did these situations cause you to believe about yourself, your worth and your value?
- How did your view of the world and yourself change after these situations?
- What are the gifts, realizations or insights you have received from changing your perspective and owning your role as a Victim?

5

V2 - VILLAIN

If - as a free thinking and free acting adult, I am the one who is making all of my own choices, choosing my own friends, writing my own story and choosing the characters and the scenery - If I am the one in charge of all of this, then who, truly, is the Villain of my story?

Villain -Noun

• A character whose evil actions or motives are important to the plot

• A person or thing responsible for specified trouble, harm or damage

• Synonyms: criminal, lawbreaker, offender, wrongdoer, con, bad guy, scoundrel

Oxford Dictionary

The Villain

I am almost always met with a little bit of resistance when I first introduce the concept of the "Villain" to my clients, especially, after we have been able to come to an understanding of what a "Victim" is in The Five Vs.

To most people, the logical thought process here is that now we are going to dissect and crucify the Villains we have identified in the previous chapter. In a way this is true, but also it isn't. Yes, we will be talking about the Villains in your life, but for the process of growth and empowerment - we will be removing all of the other players in the story except for you.

Yes, you are the only Villain we will be mainly discussing in this chapter. I acknowledge that there may have been other Villains by whom you have been Victimized. Don't feel me exonerating them here, or think I am minimizing the damage they have done, I am only working from a place where we can make real change. That place of change lies in the role you choose to own and what you choose to do with it. It is my hopes that, by the end of this chapter, you will be able to understand the role of a Villain, which you may have taken on in your own life.

This is where I usually hear such things as, "How am I the Villain now?!" I am met with anger, frustration and confusion by some - intrigue or excitement by others. But- don't throw the book away just yet. We agreed to explore these concepts together, so keep reading.

Most of my clients are not the typical Villain one would see in a movie. But some are. I want to be careful to avoid labeling the Villain as "bad," although to the outside world some may be perceived as such. In my opinion, the Villain is sick, confused or lacking their "True Truth" rather than a "bad" person. They have simply forgotten who they were at birth; the innocent child born with "pure potential" and a "clean slate."

No one is born a Victim. No one is born a Villain. We were with a perfect potential to grow as an individual in any direction we could choose. We become a Victim or Villain as a byproduct of all the experiences, rules and opinions given to us by the adults or peers around us.

If we are to follow the concept that all children are born perfect and with perfect potential, then where did the errors (the lies) creep in? Most of the time, these changes in our personal perception are introduced by the well-meaning, or not so well-meaning adults who taught us as children what was right, wrong, acceptable and unacceptable in life with their words and actions (or inactions). If a child is truly a blank slate, then all of their thoughts, habits, patterns and opinions are learned things.

So- if all of our thoughts, habits, patterns and opinions are learned things, then wouldn't it make sense that, as we travel through our lives on autopilot, we may actually be unaware of the role of Villain we may be playing in our own lives? This is important to think about; our role as "Villain" in our own life.

There are two types of Villain. The one who plays the Villain to others, and the one who plays the Villain to themselves. Every time we rob ourselves of happiness, joy, adventure, success, etc. for no good reason, we are playing the Villain towards ourselves. Every time we choose to remain in suffering, or live our lives from a place of lack and fear, we are also playing our own Villain.

Every time we rob another person of our love or hold back our Vulnerability, or the Truth, we are the Villain who chooses to keep ourselves in the state of suffering or loss of what the relationship could have been. Maybe we don't even realize we are playing the Villain, but we are. And the role of Villain is usually traded back and forth with the role of the Victim. Let me give you an example.

I am married to the most incredible man in the world. He loves me deeply and I love him. He was adopted and raised by two amazing and supportive parents in a family of amazing and supportive people.

In the beginning of our relationship, the love was there very quickly. I had done a lot of work on myself by the time this relationship showed up, but unfortunately - I wasn't aware of all of my Victim / Villain patterns yet. Neither was he. Regardless, when we got together, all seemed to go well for the first few weeks.

We met playing music. He had shown up to play the drums on a song I was recording for an album. We hit it off professionally right away. Eventually we teamed up and played music in the same band together and it was a blast.

I was already sober when we got together, but he hadn't yet found sobriety. I did my best to show up in the healthiest way, as did he. But there were patterns we both had brought into the relationship which caused us some problems. I was a Victim/Villain and so was he.

I remember that we would go play shows together and, after the shows, the band and the fans would always join up together at a local club for drinking and music that played from an incredible Juke Box with all my favorite songs.

Although I didn't drink, the bar owner was a good friend, and they always had a Cranberry- 7up waiting for me when I arrived, along with "shots" for the rest of the band. We would stay there until the place shut down, and sometimes they would keep it open just for the bands who were there to hang out after hours.

The longer we stayed, the more drunk my band members would get. After we closed down the bar, the party usually moved to my house.

Imagine coming home to my quiet house where my children were sleeping, and my neighborhood was as well. Next, imagine a living room full of musicians who have been drinking for hours coming home and continuing the party they had started after the show. To say it got loud was an understatement.

The neighbors would get angry and my children were awakened when they should have been resting for school the next day. Then, there was always the "peak" of my husband's (then still boyfriend's) night. The angry part of the night.

We laugh about the ridiculousness of it now, but at the time it wasn't very funny.

He would break up with me night after night and in the morning, he would wake up alone in the bed.

He has recounted to me that every morning he would wake up without me in bed, not remembering the night before. He would instantly be filled with a feeling of fear and dread. He knew that something must have happened the night before, but he had no recollection of what that was.

The next morning, I would be filled with the same feelings of fear and dread. But mine were for different reasons. You see, I really - really - really loved him. He was such a sweet and supportive man when he was sober. He is the most talented drummer I have ever met. He is the first man I had been able to actually fall in love with for real. By the time our relationship had started, I had done enough work on my past to be able to fall in love, and I did NOT want to lose that. So- morning after morning, I would forgive the escapades of the night before.

He would say he was sorry; I would tell him it was fine and that I loved him. I didn't want to make a boundary with him about his drinking because I was afraid he would leave me. He loved his whisky. So- I kept making sure he got it. I was a part of the problem, big time.

After a night of drinking and breaking up with me again, I would do my best to ease his guilt - but this always came after the period of silence I would make him endure before I decided to talk to him again.

Needless to say, this was not the happy, love filled scenario we have created for our marriage today.

It was not healthy for us to be choosing to participate in this night after night and I knew it.

Eventually, I had to make some choices in the relationship because deep inside of myself, I knew that our love wouldn't last if we continued with this pattern. I didn't want to be honest with how I truly felt about everything because that may mean that I might lose him. So- I lied to him over and over again and told him that I wasn't mad, and that I understood. I told him that I would stand by him "no matter what." But deep inside I feared that the relationship was doomed.

I eventually started to become unhappy. I wasn't scared of him at all because he was a gentle soul, but I was scared of what he would do the next time he got drunk.

Sober, he was the gentlest man. But when he was drunk, he was not gentle with his words at all. Keeping the story brief, my husband got sober over a decade ago after a long night out on vacation with some friends. I won't recount all of the night for you here, but it was ugly.

The next day, he woke up again to an empty bed, and this time I resolved it would stay empty. When he finally came around, he wanted to talk. I told him I was unable to speak to him without saying something I couldn't take back. I told him we were done.

It was the very first time I was truly honest with him about how I felt. But my husband, being the honest and gentle man he was, simply said to me, "You can leave me if you want, but I am done drinking. I don't want to wake up one more morning with this feeling of regret for something I don't even remember doing. I don't want to ever see someone looking at me with the eyes you are looking at me with right now. I don't know if I can stay sober on my own and you are the only sober person I know. Please stay."

Even though I was ready to leave, a little voice inside told me I should stay - if only to help this person with support as he gets sober.

He has been sober since that day and I am so incredibly glad I loved him as much as I did back then. I'm also so glad I was just co-dependent enough to not have the heart to leave him. He is my best friend and the only man who has ever loved me in the way he loves me. My husband grew up with wonderful parents who instilled an honesty inside of him that is pure and wonderful.

But back to the point of this story of the late-night partying with friends at my home and my husband's and my late-night drunken encounters followed by the next day regrets. I want you to ask yourself, right now, who is the Victim here? Who is the Villain?

There were many Victims and Villains in this scenario. Let's start with the Victims. First off, my children who also loved my husband very much. With my dishonesty, I created a situation which caused my children fear. They didn't want him to leave. They were always asking if we were going to break up. They would hear the commotion and yelling in the living room and I would have to go into the room to console them and tell them everything was okay.

In this scenario, my children were the only pure Victims. I was the Villain. The ball started rolling with me. By the choices I made, I brought in and continued to fuel an unhealthy relationship in our home which affected their security. It was my job, as a mother, to keep my children safe from anything that made them feel insecure, and my selfishness in relationships made that impossible.

Next we will look at my husband. Was he the Victim or the Villain? My husband was taken away from his birth mother at the age of one. He was taken to his adoptive family and has been loved and supported unconditionally by them ever since.

Even though he seems to have no issues with it while he

is sober, while he was drinking - it tended to come out. He would talk about why she didn't keep him and would tell me that I should just leave him because he obviously wasn't worth keeping around. It would break my heart to hear him say these things. But those feelings were there - deep down, and as an adult, the deep core belief that he wasn't worthy of keeping was present. It affected him whether he felt it or not. So- he is a Victim to those lies about his value, which caused him eventually to become the Villain of his own life. His response to them caused him to be his own Villain. He created scenarios which damaged his security and happiness.

Because of my own personal story, I made choices not to speak up in fear of being abandoned. I also made the choice not to speak up because I had a problem breaking up with people. I was always afraid deep down that anyone I broke up with could potentially react in the same way my ex did so I stayed past the normal time a healthy person would have stayed.

I kept important information from him and told him lies when I said he was ok. I would tell him I loved him, and he didn't do anything wrong. I would flip flop back and forth between telling him I was okay with the night before and telling him I wanted him to do better. I was never direct with my message. I never asked him to quit drinking. He never REALLY had my truth.

Without truth, how was a person supposed to show up the way I needed him to? I was the Villain because I chose comfort over truth. I chose to allow a lie to remain in between us which would eventually bring the end of our relationship. Had that relationship failed, it would have been my doing because I couldn't be totally honest. I was my own Villain as well because I was sabotaging any chance at happiness with my inability to state my truth. So- in theory, I was also my own Victim.

It's important for me to own the Villain role in this scenario, for it is truly where my empowerment comes into play. If I remain the Victim in my mind, then I am stating that other people are responsible for my happiness and unhappiness. There is no solution if I remain in the role of the Victim. I can only change my circumstances by being in the role of "responsibility", aka, owning my role as my own Villain.

As a child, I was the Victim - but if I am continuing to be unhappy and choose to live an existence where my happiness depends on the choices and actions of others, eventually I have to look in the mirror for change. I can blame my inability to make boundaries in a relationship on the fact I was beaten and had a man shoot himself in front of me all I want. But if I am no longer with the person I am blaming my behavioral patterns on now, well then who is in charge? If I choose to stay in a place where I am unhappy, then I am the Villain. The one who forces their "way" on someone is the Villain. If I choose to remain under someone else's control, or if I relinquish the right to my own happiness to appease someone else's wants or needs, that is MY choice. I can only blame my choices on me. It's called "owning my Truth." If I choose to sacrifice myself or my happiness for others, whether it be for a noble cause or not – it is MY choice to do so. At any time, I am free to make a different choice. If I do choose to make a different choice, I am still the one making the choice. Regardless of whether or not someone else has a role in my choices, they are still MINE. Once I can own those choices, I have at least started to regain my personal power and am now moving forward to my True Truth – or my authentic Vested Self.

Yes, the things I went through when I was younger were terrible. But as an adult, I have free reign to keep choosing those who are the players in my life. The patterns that a Victim carries into their future are countless. We cannot afford to remain in those patterns.

A child who was made to feel small and worthless by an adult will often subconsciously do the same to themselves or those around them as an adult. If a child is laughed at or made to look silly when they dance, then as an adult they may choose to never dance in public for fear of looking stupid or being laughed at.

If a teacher tells a child they think they have a learning deficiency, that child may carry this learned truth into their adult life and, even then, continue to believe themselves to have a learning deficiency. They may carry it on into adulthood telling themselves internally that they believe they are stupid, without having any supporting evidence.

If a child is told they are too needy, they may refuse to ask for love or support as an adult. They may blame their failed relationships on their parents, or past relationships and even sound very justified for being afraid of asking for love or support. But while blaming their present behavior on the words or actions of others, they are still faced with the simple fact that they are the one running the show. They may have been molded in to thinking they were needy or unlovable as a child, but who is now saying these things to them? They are saying these things to themselves and making choices based on these fears and beliefs.

We repeat the same words that we are taught to think about ourselves, our value and our rights well into adulthood. We go from being the Victim as a child to being our own Villain as an adult. We don't give up on what we are taught.

When I started writing this book, I was faced with the desire to cover each "V" from as many angles as I could contrive so that as many people as possible would find their place of identification. It feels difficult to explain in simple terms since there are so many different levels of Villainous actions. There are the obvious versus the not so obvious examples (the easy to spot versus deeply hidden behaviors and choices). That's the thing with the Five V's. They are not discernible unless you really think about them and you have to be in a place of understanding where you can safely take an up close and personal look at yourself. You have to be willing to be open to what you might find. It can be like walking a tight rope, but it can be done and your reward, in the end, is priceless.

When I was a child my hero was Wonder Woman. I was mesmerized by her bravery and wished so much that I could borrow the "lasso of truth" that she wielded. Any bad guy she caught would be detained and then she would wrap the lasso of truth around them and they were compelled to tell the truth, the whole truth, and nothing but the truth. I would sit and watch that television show and wish I could find my own lasso of truth to come and save me from the secrets I was hiding from myself. As I got older, I didn't necessarily want Wonder Woman to save me, I wanted to be capable of being my own hero in my own mind. I thought, if only I had my own lasso of truth! If only I had the right tools.

As I said earlier, I began reading self-help books at a young age. I began to gather tools (lassos) in the books I read. I found many "Truths" about myself and the resulting happiness to which every human being is entitled to. These "Truths" started setting me free. This book is actually intended to be, in theory, a lasso of truth for you to use.

I must point out, though, that while the "Truth" is something that can set you free when you finally embrace it, it is also very difficult for many of us to accept sole responsibility for our circumstances. But-the Truth is the Truth, whether you can see it now or not. At some point in life, if we do not acknowledge our responsibility in these circumstances, those who are Victimized will purposely or unconsciously fall into the role of being their own Villain.

If you haven't figured it out yet, YOU are the one and only person who has the greatest ability to be the "Hero" or "Villain" of your own life adventure. Whether or not you are currently feeling empowered is all in your hands. Some of us may have been victimized by random crime or someone else's choices. But, if you have chosen to allow yourself to be Victimized by another and you are not doing anything to help yourself out of it, you have now, essentially, become your own Villain. If you want to feel empowered, to be your own "Hero," it is your absolute right and responsibility to do this. If you are not interested or ready to take action on your own behalf, my heart goes out to you. But, no one can help you make changes, take actions or make decisions that you do not want to make. The choice lies with you.

You can recognize when a Victim "thought pattern"

resides in your mind by paying attention to your words, thoughts and actions (or inactions). As long as you are thinking like a Victim, you will act in the way a Victim acts. If someone believes there is no way out of a situation, they will not try very hard to get out. An empowered person knows that there is always a way out of the Victim mindset. There may have been horrible circumstances in your childhood or you past. Even now there may be horrible circumstances in your life – YOU are the only one who can make the choice to remain in the place of a "Victim" in your own mind. You are the only one who can stop yourself from being the Villain right now. Yes, if you are allowing yourself to be damaged by current people, places or situations – you are the Villain – acting against yourself.

I am not passing judgment. As an adult I have been in situations therein which it seemed impossible to leave even if I had wanted to. But I was the one who chose to stay. I was the Villain who now continued to tell myself I deserved this and allow myself to stay in situations which reinforced the thought that I wasn't worthy of anything better. I wasn't purposely wanting to harm myself by my choices, I simply didn't think there was any other alternative. I wish I would've known what I know now. But that is why I am sharing this with you. Just in case you are stuck in that same cycle of unhappiness or held hostage by your own fears, I want you to know there are an infinite number of alternative options available right now, and there is always a way out.

I also tread lightly around the area of people who have been a Victim of violence or sexual assault as I have. I was not the 'Villain' in those situations - but I found that after I had some distance between myself and that moment, I made choices to shut people out, withhold my love, be angry at myself and mean to those who tried to help me. The more I kept myself from connecting to others around me, or refused to allow myself to be happy, the more of a Villain I became to those who wanted to love me and to myself who deserved to be happy and free of pain.

I have been a Villain in the way I have treated myself, as well. I have spoken to myself in a way that has negated my value, my basic rights and my worth. Looking back at the times I was the Villain of my own story, I now know that if I had told other people the things that I was saying to myself, I'm sure that anyone in their right mind would have told me to STOP LISTENING TO THAT PERSON! I would have told someone to stop listening to the things I was saying if they were speaking to themselves that way as well. It is much more difficult to see how horrible you are being when it is you, talking to yourself, withholding love from yourself and blocking your own happiness.

When I was younger, I created a "personal rule" for my own safety, which I committed to live by; Don't let anyone in until I'm sure they are safe. Because of this personal inner law I adopted for myself, it has always taken a while for me to deeply connect with other people. As much as I would have liked to have been the happy go lucky person I put myself out there and pretended to be, friendship, love and commitment scared me. I would have a group of friends, or one on one friendships, but as soon as I felt them getting too close, I ghosted them and got a new set of friends.

My decision as a child to keep my heart guarded was a hard habit to break. You see, when I was little, I was a fearless child. I remember being that way. But as I learned about adults and their ways of lying and deceiving each other, as well as what they had done to me, I learned to be weary and afraid of everyone. Human connection scared me. Adults scared me.

Because of the rash decisions of my ex-boyfriend and his final violent reaction of committing suicide in front of me, I was left emotionally scarred. I didn't trust that any of the reactions of other people were going to be safe ones. So, learning to speak up for myself was a painfully hard skill to develop.

As I began my healing process, it got easier. But even after years of healing, it sometimes still took a lot for me to speak up when I felt hurt, slighted or offended. Each time I interacted with people in these seemingly hard situations, I knew I had the choice of either playing a Victim, becoming a Villain, or finding a way to bring the True Truth of love and healing in. I learned that regardless of how the other person acted or reacted, it was neither here nor there, I was the one experiencing MY SIDE. I had to make the choice of how I was going to react.

I remember having an argument with a friend once, that wasn't really an argument at all, but we'll call it that for purposes of this story. I was doing a weekly project that was very near and dear to my heart with him and another friend.

While I was on vacation for one week, I was unable to be there for the taping of the show. My normal spot on camera was filled with another woman and my friend accidentally stated that I had been "replaced" with this other woman. Even though it was an innocent statement, the way he stated it appeared to say that there was an "unspoken" situation that had happened and that I was "permanently replaced." Which wasn't the case.

My ego flared up big time. I was so embarrassed. I knew he didn't mean for it to sound that way, but to me, what he had said sounded like it would give our audience the idea that I had to be replaced for some unsaid reason. The more I thought about it the more I wanted to make sure that the next time I went on vacation, they stated I was only on vacation.

I went to him and asked if I could talk to him honestly about something that was bothering me before we did our next show. Normally, I would have chosen to just keep silent, but I felt it really deep in my heart; I needed to speak up about it.

Logically, I recognized that my ego felt slighted, but the

project meant a lot to me and it hurt to ignore it. I wanted to see if it could be handled differently next time. I didn't want to carry ill feelings toward him. I figured we were both close enough friends that he would understand how it sounded and it would be no big deal. As I showed up to his house to work on the project, we proceeded to have our conversation.

I could tell immediately that he felt embarrassed when he realized what he had done. I have known this man for over a decade and I know that he cannot stomach being the "Villain" in any situation. I recognize it because I too am the same way.

As he became the Villain of this scenario more and more in his head, he became angrier and angrier with me. He then started pointing the finger back at me and stating things that I have done in the past that he perceived as offensive. I acknowledged and apologized for my past actions and I did my best to speak lovingly about the situation but as the conversation went forward it started to spiral out of control in a direction neither of us intended for it to go.

My friend escalated his screaming at me and threw me out of his house. I left of course. Completely blindsided by what had just happened. Confused as to how it went that direction. We had always been so open and honest with each other. I also knew that he was going through a hard time in life at that moment and his reaction was probably not all about me. I love this man like he is my brother and I knew inside that he loved me like I was his sister.

This was the pivotal moment where I was acutely aware that I could choose to be the Victim. It was the point where I could choose to be the Villain as well.

I had the choice not to take it personal and to just allow him his space to feel whatever it was he was feeling and work through it. I knew inside how much we loved each other, in spite of the current situation. You'd think, being a spiritual teacher and life coach that I would have chosen to bring love into the experience.

Instead, I chose to become the Villain in this story. I went at it full board. I chose to listen to my head; the part where my ego resides. I gave power to the part of me that likes to play Judge, Jury and Executioner. I became the Villain.

My ego (a tool of the Villain) spoke so loud to me at that

moment, insisting that I make a conscious choice to "assign the role of Villain" to someone, and it wasn't going to be me! So, I decided to assign the role of "Villain" to my friend.

I took away his right to be upset and I handled the situation poorly by choosing to assign him the role of my "Villain" for all of it. I immediately took action. I blocked his number in my phone so that when the time came when I knew he would apologize; I wouldn't be available to take the phone call. I blocked him on all of our social media feeds so that he couldn't see my posts. I also made a decision that he was not going to see me be "weak." I would "show him."

I love this friend like he is my own family. I knew in my gut that I was choosing to punish him and that I was wrong, but I didn't choose to stop. Sometimes playing the role of the Villain can seem justified and powerful.

That is the usual way I act out and punish people, by the way. I remove myself from their life and make myself unavailable to them at all. I kill the relationship. I become the "Villain" by ruining my own connections with other people. I no longer need the other person to hurt me, because I do it for them by cutting off what could have been a lifelong friendship. I play the Villain by closing off the connection. I make a conscious (sometimes unconscious) choice of hurting both of us on purpose by taking that action.

Thank God for the Five Vs that I was now teaching to others. I couldn't be a teacher in this concept and not take my own advice.

So, I had an obligation to look at the situation again. Not from the vantage point of a Victim, but rather from the empowered place of owning my role as a Villain in my own scenario that I had created. It wasn't easy.

The ego is a powerful and sneaky thing when it rears its ugly head. So, I had to find and remain in the True Truth. I had to ask myself, "If this was a perfect world and this situation had gone perfectly, what would the outcome be?"

Well, in a perfect world, the outcome would have been that our friendship would still be intact, and we would still feel deep love in our hearts for each other. So, there it was, I had a choice to make.

Would I remain in the role of a Villain, allowing this friendship to end? Or would I get to the True Truth? The

True Truth which was the fact that my ego was involved, and I never wanted to live a day without him in my life. So, I went at the situation with those True Truths in mind.

In the end, this situation turned out to be a deep and powerful experience for both of us. Once I acknowledged the Visceral Reaction to where our situation had traveled, I checked through the checklist of the Five Vs and chose to heal instead of continuing on the path I was on.

I got into the "True Truth" about who and what we were in this existence. I chose to love instead of losing.

My friend never had a clue that I had experienced any of these feelings until I read this part of the chapter to him over the phone. We discussed the fact that we both had such an opportunity to Victimize this beautiful friendship and we thanked the Universe that we so quickly were able to become Vulnerable and heal.

I also told him that since his daughter is my goddaughter and was named after me, it was probably a good idea I didn't leave him with a resentment that would ruin the name for him. We laughed. That's the beautiful thing about bringing these teachings into our life. We can use them in such beautiful ways.

It is important to be able to recognize when we are in each of the Five V's as well. We can derail a potential emotional train wreck with just a little bit of reflection, love and action.

This is not the only area of life that I have been the Villain though. I have been the Villain in other areas as well. I have Victimized others I felt threatened by with words meant to invoke fear or insecurity in them. I also have done this with actual actions of aggression and physical violence towards others in the past. I cringed as I wrote that last part. Because that is not who I am in my heart of hearts. I love my fellow human being and my intention is always to heal and never to hurt others.

But the True Truth is that over my lifetime, when dealing with others, ego and fear have caused me to "strike first" before they had a chance to. I have been my own Villain, as well, victimizing myself and my partners by continuing to stay in relationships where I wasn't in love at all because I was afraid to break up with them due to my past break up experience. I selfishly stole time from their life which could have been dedicated to someone who truly would have loved them as any human deserved to be loved. I chose to stay, whether out of fear, or laziness, or even because of a deep need to prove I was a good person.

The "True Truth" is that I was the person who made the choice to stay in those circumstances. I made the choice to keep my heart shielded from others so they couldn't hurt me.

I chose to stay in a dead-end job because I was afraid to take any risks.

I chose to take less than I deserved because "at least I was getting something."

I chose to give up on my dreams in the name of "being realistic."

This list could go on and on... but every time I kept myself from thriving or being happy in life, I was playing the Villain in my own story.

And, as much as I don't want it to be true, I became the Villain many times in other people's story as well.

I shamed my own children for asking so much of me when from my point of view, having numerous jobs at once, all I did was work to support them.

I refused to be completely Vulnerable in relationships to keep from being hurt in the end.

I stole job opportunities from others in the name of being a 'good mother' and 'seizing opportunity.'

I have physically and verbally assaulted people who have hurt my feelings or my pride.

I have been cold when someone needed love.

I have played the Villain in so many ways that I do not believe I could ever finish the list.

I have unfairly altered the happiness and potential happiness of others by ignoring the "right thing to do" while I had the chance to take action. **WHICH, IN TURN**, has caused me to **BECOME MY OWN VILLAIN OR A VILLAIN TO OTHERS** by drowning myself in guilt, shame and self-hatred for my actions (and inactions). As I reflected, I would re-live the experiences and then had to figure out a way that I could feel justified. So, I blamed everyone else and refused to take responsibility or action to change the circumstances – choosing to stay in the Victim or Villain role.

I chose these roles, creating from this a perpetual cycle of Victim / Villain / Victim / Villain / Victim... ad nauseam.

If you have been able to see the pattern of Victim/Villain for yourself, this is wonderful. In order for you to get yourself out of this kind of thinking, you will first need to see where playing the Victim or Villain does not serve you. Then you will need a very clear idea of where you are thinking or acting yourself into these roles. We do this bravely without judgement of ourselves or the other players. Judgment only keeps us stuck. We do this by mustering up as much forgiveness as we can find inside us. Even if it is only a little seed of forgiveness, this is still a great start. Everyone has made mistakes in action or judgements. We do not reflect or dwell for too long on the fact we have been wrong. In staying stuck in blame, we always result in getting caught in the Victim / Villain trap again. Please give yourself a break at this time. Beating yourself up defeats the purpose of the realizations you have made thus far.

Do not worry. Becoming aware of your own potential to play the Villain is actually empowering in the end. You will find, the most important part of Villain awareness is being able to recognize when you are tempted to adopt that role for yourself.

ANYTHING THAT HARMS, ROBS OR HINDERS YOURSELF OR SOMEONE ELSE OF HAPPINESS, JOY, OR EMPOWERMENT IS YOU PLAYING THE VILLAIN.

ANY TIME YOU ARE THE VILLAIN - YOU ARE ALSO YOUR OWN VICTIM.

It is pretty obvious that neither of those roles are conducive to a happy and productive life. So, once you become aware that you are playing the Victim or Villain– it is important that you immediately get into a solution. How? Well, the first step I would suggest, as I have mentioned above, is to search for a place to offer forgiveness for all people involved. I do this sometimes by trying to imagine what they must have to think or feel inside, what situations may have happened in their past to make them feel the need to play the Victim or Villain in their own lives. I make an effort to see that they were not born as Victims or Villains, that just like myself – they learned to play those roles. Most important here, though, is becoming aware of your own Visceral vibration (your inner discomfort). Make it a point to notice when this Visceral reaction shows up. Acknowledge the thoughts inside, feel how it is sparked and quiet your mind enough to listen to what your body is TRYING TO TELL YOU. Yes, become aware of your body trying to communicate with you. How do you become aware? We will be discussing that next with the 3rd "V" – Visceral.

Let's Contemplate "Villain"

QUESTIONS TO ASK YOURSELF ABOUT PLAYING YOUR OWN ROLE AS A VILLAIN.

- Where have you become the Villain in your own life towards yourself?
- Where have you been the Villain towards others?
- Where have you robbed yourself of happiness?
- Where have you robbed others of enjoying life?
- Where have you allowed a "lie" to exist when the "truth" was uncomfortable?
- Where are you unwilling or unable to forgive yourself?
- What were you taught about people, love, the world, abundance, and Vulnerability as a child?
- How might you be if you hadn't been taught the negative things you were taught as a child?

6

V3 - VISCERAL

Visceral - adjective

• Relating to the viscera, the internal organs in the body, especially the gut or intestines.

• Relating to deep inward feelings rather than to the intellect

Synonyms: instinctive, instinctual, gut, deep-down, deep-seated, inward, emotional, deep-rooted

Oxford Dictionary

We have done a lot of discussing of the Victim and the Villain, we can now understand that when we are in those roles, we are held hostage to beliefs and values which were crafted from the past that are actively shaping current and future experiences. We cannot change the past, but we can change the "now" experiences we are having. Excluding an act of Violence or Tyranny, the choice to be a Victim or Villain is always made in the "now". It is always preceded by a feeling which stems from fear. This feeling is a Visceral feeling.

VISCERAL IS ALWAYS EXPERIENCED IN THE "NOW".

At every moment of every day, I am being spoken to Viscerally by my body. It is a string of messages from deep within. I feel them as a "knowing", "deep intuition", "twinge of excitement" or a "disturbance" inside. I may think that a Visceral discomfort comes from thoughts of the past or worries about the future. But the truth is that my Visceral reaction is always affected by my PRESENT thoughts, feelings and fears. When I feel disturbed, it is because there is an absence of truth somewhere in my life and I know I will continue to feel "Viscerally Disturbed" until I find that lie and correct it. When I am feeling "Viscerally Calm or Inspired" it is because I am in a place of "True Truth" inside. While taking actions viewing the outside circumstance with the "True Truth," I can then create from an empowered place.

In the preceding chapters we have spoken about the

Victim and the Villain roles and what happens when we are trapped by the thought patterns and mindsets that are born from those experiences. But now I want to bring you to something we will call acting in "the NOW". When we explore the 3rd V which is Visceral, this is always experienced in the HERE and NOW. Even when we are replaying or entertaining a personal scenario in our mind, we may think we are experiencing a Visceral reaction to those particular past or future thoughts or experiences. This is not true. Even though these may be past moments, the Visceral feeling we are experiencing is currently happening in the NOW. Our Visceral reaction is being affected by current thoughts and feelings. For example, my mother and I have done a lot of healing between us. In the beginning of us becoming reconnected – I would have a very strong Visceral reaction whenever she would call to talk to me on the phone. I would think to myself that I was having this Visceral reaction inside because of the things that happened in the past. But the True Truth was that I had these Visceral reactions because I still felt unimportant or worthless inside about myself when she called. I was having these disturbing Visceral reactions because I had not changed my current thoughts about myself yet.

When we had healed our relationship, and I discovered how truly important and lovable I was, the Visceral reaction to my mother's calls changed. Now when she calls, I get a very positive and excited Visceral reaction inside. My NOW thoughts are different, so my NOW Visceral reaction is different too. My Visceral reaction never had anything to do with anyone else, my Visceral feelings were always sparked by how I felt about myself in the NOW. We can no longer go back or forward in time to change the situations which are still somehow affecting our life experience. If we pay attention to our Visceral reaction, we can do some investigation and find out what current thoughts, beliefs or fears are still causing any negative Visceral reactions. We find out what the True Truth about ourselves, this world and our experiences truly are, and we can also find out what is standing in the way of our inner peace. I want you to open your mind up as we dive into this next section of this book. I want you to open up your heart as well. Most importantly, I want you to reach down past the mind and your heart and into your "Gut." Why the gut, you ask? Because the easiest place to quickly feel and recognize a Visceral reaction happening is in the "Gut."

Although I have just recently been made aware of

something called the "Gut-Brain Connection," I have never been taught about them. The study says there are two Brains in our body which are constantly present and reacting to our outer stimuli as well as inner thoughts, which I agree with. But I think it goes a bit further than that. I have come to my own theory that there are more than just these two Brains. I believe there are many more parts of our body that communicate and help us in our decision making. In this book, I will focus on the three brains which I work with my clients on the most. I have a theory that these three brains are always pining for our attention to help us make decisions which will help us stay safe. So, I would like to speak a bit about this theory with you, which are not based solely on scientific "facts," but more on "personal experiences."

I BELIEVE WE HAVE "3 BRAINS"

1.   Our Head

2.   Our Heart

3.   Our Gut

1.   Our Head Brain. This is the place where our logic and opinions reside. It is also the place our ego resides. The head Brain is always reminding us of our rules and is always talking to us about our decisions and judgments. This Brain has a memory of "the perceived facts" and all the stories you tell yourself. The purpose of the ego portion of this Brain is to "protect you" - or so it tells itself. The head brain is the brain which assigns the roles of Victim and Villain and is more than happy to present us with facts that support us staying in those roles.

2.   The Heart Brain. This is the place where our conscious emotions reside; our wants and our desires. This Brain is where passion and desire are emitted. The purpose of this Brain is to emotionally attach us to the world around us. This is the brain which feels the pain of loss and joy of life. It experiences the pain which leads to the feeling of being a Victim. Concurrently, the head brain is extremely protective of this brain.

3.   Our Gut Brain. Your gut is the "knowing" area of your body: The part that feels the vibration of everything and everyone around you. Sometimes your gut feels very heavy and other times it feels light; Not in

the gravitational sense but in the emotional sense. When our Gut Brain is talking to us, we feel it deep down as a Visceral vibration or an intuitive "knowing" which doesn't come from either of the other two Brains. The purpose of this Brain is intuition and it is where the "True Truth" resides. It is the most ignored, or untapped Brain, but it is always working, and we can always feel it, whether we are aware of it or not.

It is in this 3rd V, "Visceral" – led by the Gut Brain, that I want you to now try to connect. If you are not sure how to connect with this Brain, or how to feel it, that's ok. We will discuss it in this chapter.

Have you ever walked into a room and had a sinking feeling that something wasn't "quite right" in that room or felt the feeling of anticipation deep inside, like something was about to happen? Have you ever met someone new and felt a special connection with them knowing you had never met them in person before? Have you ever intuitively known the answer to something that you know you had no way of knowing?

The Gut is where those feelings come from and that is the place I want to connect you with.

It has been said that your Gut is the more dominant Brain in the body, we have just been taught or have decided to ignore it and trust the Brain upstairs more. The problem with the Brain upstairs is that it can have two different stories, or a few different versions of a situation all happening and fighting with each other at one time.

The Head Brain can tell us lies and manipulate the truth. The Heart Brain doesn't discern between right and wrong. It just wants what it wants without much logic. So- it cannot always be trusted either. The Gut Brain is where your "knowing that you know" comes from. The Gut Brain can be relied on as the "current" indicator of your present peace of mind with any experience, situation or opinion. It always operates in the NOW. Your Gut Brain is unable to tell lies. The Gut Brain causes your whole body to fire up Viscerally.

Let's take a moment to explore each of these Brains individually.

I want you to stop for a moment after you read each paragraph below. You can either put this book down, or just simply close your eyes. I want you to listen to your different Brains as they speak to you.

First, I want you to be still and listen to your Head Brain. Think about the first person who comes to mind. Think about someone you love or think about someone you do not like. Do you hear all of the thoughts running around in your head? Do you hear the analyzation of those thoughts? Next, do you also hear the analyzation of the analyzation of those thoughts?

We could spend hours, days and even months following the direction of thought after thought about what we are thinking in our Head Brain.

Now let's pay a little attention to your Heart Brain. I like to joke that this is our "cute little child-like Brain," void of too many opinions. It just sits there waiting for something to pique its attention. Think again about someone you really love. Do you feel the swelling of emotion in your heart? And now think about someone you lost that you still long for. Do you feel that as well?

The Heart Brain is an innocent, childlike Brain who receives more information than it chooses to give. It takes thoughts and opinions of the Head Brain and the Gut Brain into account. It rarely works without the other two Brains giving input to it.

But when working autonomously, the Heart Brain desires and it aches, depending on the outside stimulus. When we fall in love, it desires more. When we lose love, it breaks and feels the loss.

Now stop again and pay attention to your Gut Brain. In order to connect with this, we will use the body as a whole. This time I want you to feel the feelings that you are experiencing deep inside at this very moment.

Do you feel calm?

Do you feel uneasy?

Is there a tightness in your gut or body at all?

Now I want you to think about someone you love. Can you feel the change?

Now I want you to think about someone you don't particularly like. Think about your bills. Think about your job. Think about your family. Think about being on time to catch a flight and traffic on the way to the airport. How does your Gut Brain (which often affects your entire body) Viscerally react to these different thoughts?

At every moment of every day, we have a Visceral

reaction happening inside of our body. Our Gut Brain sends a Visceral vibration through our body as it reacts to Truths and Falsities. When it is misaligned, when there is a lie about ourselves and our worth, or there is a lack of truth in the things we are experiencing, our Gut Brain vibrates a feeling of "there is something wrong," and we feel it as discomfort, uneasiness, pending doom or irritation. We sometimes react so strongly that we get sick, throw up or experience other physical reactions.

When it is aligned (or in the True Truth), it is calm and there is a "sense" of "knowing" that we experience. Don't worry if you haven't mastered the ability to identify your gut reactions at this time, you will. For now, I simply want you to be open to the following facts:

Fact #1.

Every single one of us has a gut reaction to our inner dialogue and our outer circumstances. It is happening all the time, at every moment of every day.

Fact #2.

Most of us have trained ourselves to ignore our gut feelings, thus ignoring what's happening Viscerally inside of ourselves. We ignore the messages from our gut and take opposing actions to make others comfortable, make ourselves fit in, and follow the rules set down for us by the humans that exist around us.

Fact #3.

Lies and confusion are the number one culprit of negative Visceral states. Being unauthentic sets this off. Lies and inauthenticity are killers of our soul.

Fact #4.

When we constantly ignore our Gut Brain and allow confusion, mistruths or deviation to continue to exist, we can become physically or emotionally ill.

AUTHENTICITY: This is a very important word that I will discuss for a brief moment here. The word authentic means to be "of genuine quality," "not fake or false."

In my teachings, I use the word Authenticity quite often because it is a place that most, if not all of my students are looking to achieve inside themselves. When we can find a place of "Authenticity," it is something that cannot be shaken. It is where the "Vested Self Truths" reside. I will talk about this more in the Fifth V, but for now, I wanted you to have a benchmark to identify the discomfort in our Visceral place with. This is one of the most important tools you will be able to master, identifying a negative or unwanted Visceral reaction. Most of the time, this is pinged by something which is not authentic. A lie about ourselves, others or a situation we are a party to or observing.

When we are being unauthentic, our body creates a Visceral reaction alerting us that we are experiencing a lack of truth going on somewhere in our life. We get the message that "something is not right." Once this happens, most of us have been trained to immediately consult our head to ask what the proper thoughts or actions should be in order for us to remain a "the good guy." In order for us to "justify" our behavior, action, or lack of action, we have been trained to push our Visceral Reaction to the side and go with our Head's reaction. For example, when we know that we are being the Villain in a situation, but are not interested in being accountable to that role, we will ignore the Visceral reaction inside so that we do not have to feel the guilt, shame or hurt we are causing. We return to the head brain to justify our actions – we assign ourselves the role of Victim, or assign others the role of Villain. But the

Visceral reaction, although it can be quieted, never shuts down. It just sits there, sending out uncomfortable feelings and waiting to be acknowledged again.

Sometimes this Visceral reaction shows up as a gnawing feeling in my gut. I give this Visceral feeling different labels at different times. Sometimes I call it my "I know that I know" feeling. Other times I will refer to it as my "warning signals." I will also refer to my gut as the place where my intuition and alignment with Source stems from.

When I am making a complete assessment of my present Visceral state, I will take into account many different factors. When you start doing this, it may feel a little bit foreign. Some people will even state, "I don't think I have a Visceral reaction that I'm aware of." Don't worry, you do - and I have already begun to show you how to tap into it in this chapter.

When I was a child and I was being abused, no one had ever told me that what that man was doing to me was wrong. On the contrary, I was taught to "respect my elders" in a way that meant that an adult could do no wrong. They were ALWAYS right. I remember feeling inside that something was "off" about the interactions between this man and myself.

It wasn't as though I had a personal knowledge that it was bad. No one but this man and I knew what was going on, so no one had ever said to me, "Hey, when that man touches you in a way that makes you feel icky-it's not normal, or good, or right." But I did have this deep Visceral reaction inside that it was wrong. When I was around that man and he would look at me 'in a certain way', I would have a deep reaction in my gut that disturbed me.

The moment my mother asked me about it there were many warning signals that went off in my body. Fear, dread, doom… and a deep Visceral reaction that told me it was right to tell on him. In my gut, "I knew that I knew" that I needed to say something.

During the years of working through my emotional destruction, and in the middle of all the internal pain I was feeling- there was always this deep (and I mean DEEP) seated feeling that I shouldn't be so sad. I was supposed to be happy. I didn't know why that felt so true to me, but it was there. I mostly felt it when I looked at other people who were hurting or being harmed. For myself, it was always hard to admit that anyone else was doing something wrong. But when I saw others struggling, I knew deep inside that it wasn't right.

When I first got into recovery, I found my way in to a group that had many members who had been sober for significant amounts of time. I remember walking into my very first meeting. I was scared and miserable. I looked around the room at these happy, connected people smiling at each other and laughing out loud.

My Head Brain started talking to me, saying things like, "I don't belong here." My Head Brain was always talking. It never seemed to shut up. It was always sharing with me what it thought "our" opinion should be in any situation. But no matter how loud my Head continued to speak and try to get me to leave, deep down Viscerally, I heard the message my body was giving to me from the core of my being and it said, "you're going to be okay if you stay here." I figured that I could stay for a little while and see what happened.

While my head was telling me I wasn't worth it and I should just leave, that no one cares about me and that my life had been destroyed, my Gut was always there quietly reminding me that there was another truth: The True Truth. I deserved to be happy, joyous and free.

When these lies were created by my ego in my Head Brain, I would feel the fight between these thoughts wrestling with something deep inside of my viscera.

I know that same fight is there for many others too. If not, why would anyone even bother reading self-help books, or working out, or eating better? Why would anyone make life changes if there wasn't an internal "knowing" that we are supposed to be healthy? A "knowing" that we were born to be healthy, happy, prosperous and joyous.

When I first started discussing "Visceral Awareness" with my clients and students, I felt compelled to make this the first V, because it is often the first "gauge" we have in identifying where there is a lie being paid attention to in our life. It is the Visceral discomfort which isolates an area in which we may need to make a change in our life. It is the first thing I ask my students to pay attention to throughout the day. Their Visceral state as they carry on will be affected by their inner dialogue, thoughts and surroundings. But it soon became apparent that the Victim and the Villain needed to be addressed first in order to make headway with Visceral. The student needed to understand that they were playing the role of Victim and Villain in their lives first. From that Victim / Villain awareness, they would have a base of understanding of the damage those roles play in their lives. They needed to be aware of this before we could work with "the feelings of the Visceral" and go forward. Thus, Visceral is the 3rd "V".

Our current Visceral state is a perfect indicator of where we are presently at emotionally. Ask yourself right now, "WHAT IS MY CURRENT VISCERAL FEELING?" The Visceral feeling you are experiencing in the NOW is caused by your CURRENT thoughts and beliefs about yourself and the world. If you can be consciously aware of what thoughts are causing this Visceral reaction, and then use the Five V's in the way described in this book, you can free yourself from the trap of the lies your head is holding you hostage to.

As children, when we are being taught how to behave - we are groomed to ignore our feelings and become "logical" about things. Logic resides in our Head Brain. As I said before, it is where our ego works from. It is the "chess player" and the "observer." Our Head Brain is like a computer drive that holds all of the files containing the rules and judgments of others and ourselves. It is like an internal score card, always taking notes and strategizing. This Brain is usually the loudest opponent I come up against when helping people get out of the Victim /Villain mindset. We often have to find a "logical reason" for there to be a change that can be accepted by our Head Brain.

The Heart is usually the quietest Brain in the beginning. After all, hasn't so much of this work been done to protect our heart from being hurt? The heart is where our dreams and desires reside (most of which we have silenced, hidden or imprisoned by the time we reach our teenage years).

The Gut, however, is sneaky and wise for it is ALWAYS working to let us know where we stand as far as our **"Authenticity"** goes.

We can always tell which Brain is in charge by our words:

"My head tells me that... "

"I know in my heart that... "

"I can feel it in my gut..."

Our body works together with its three brains, working

in unison to make our decisions and keeping us preserved in safety.

We can shut our head off and ignore our thoughts - we can shut our heart off and put armor on to protect ourselves... But our Gut is ALWAYS speaking to us. Always on, always communicating. Even if we are unaware of it or refuse to listen.

When all three of them (the Head, the Heart and the Gut) are aligned, we feel the most at peace.

When we feel something is totally right; when we are being truly authentic in our "True Truth," when we are "Sure we are sure we are sure....," our whole body gets to feeling a Visceral reaction which is calm – we are "Aligned." It fires up with a feeling of surety.

THIS IS EXCITING AND SO VERY POWERFUL!

When we are operating on a lie, or an untruth, there is a Visceral uneasiness which can be ignored, but not shut off.

THIS IS WHAT YOU WANT TO LEARN TO BE AWARE OF!

As children we are conditioned to "think and act

rationally" and "be realistic." This behavior is regulated by our Head Brain. Conditioning has caused us to ignore the Gut and instead, readjust our behavior based on the opinions we have been given by others (which we have adopted as our own). Those opinions are constantly playing and re-playing in our head. We ignore the Visceral messages from our Gut and behave in a way that will gain us acceptance from others.

For many of my newer students, ignoring their gut has been so entrained in their behavior, that they are not consciously aware that the Visceral discomfort is even happening until we connect to it.

As a way to connect with your Visceral being, your Gut Brain, try this: Take the time to really observe yourself during your day to day life, maybe even set a timer to sneak up on your Visceral state of being. For times when you are aware of a strong Visceral Reaction, stop and ask yourself what is going on around you currently, or what your brain is telling you about yourself that is causing you to have this Visceral reaction. Then ask yourself if there is a lie being entertained by your Head Brain, "Is there a lie going on here causing me to have this feeling?" Then ask yourself, "What is the True Truth about this thought?" Is this lie about myself based in the reality that everyone deserves happiness, joy, love and empowerment? If it is not, align yourself with the empowering thoughts – even returning to when you were born. If you were born perfect and with pure potential, then you are still that person. Maybe some thoughts have been implanted in your head by others about your value – or maybe you have experienced some unfair treatment, but the treatment or opinion of others doesn't change who you were born to be. They simply have confused you and caused you to believe their version of the truth. Get rid of the story others have sold you about yourself and reclaim your "Authentic Self." If you have made poor choices in the past, do your best to remember who you were born to be. You are still that person underneath all of the extra baggage you have collected over time. For those of us who have regained the empowered self, we can face almost any circumstance as our Vested self – and our Visceral state will not be disturbed.

At every moment of every day OUR Visceral REACTION to our present thoughts and/or circumstances is happening, and THAT is what I want you to look for and be consistently aware of.

When going through their day, I tell my clients to check in with their "Visceral Alignment" and see if they can detect any disturbance. If there is any feeling of uneasiness, we must first ask ourselves where it is that we are now "out of Truth" "What is causing me to have this feeling?" What is the True Truth?" Here is a guide to getting the answers:

We start with...

Am I being a Victim?

Am I being a Villain?

What is the "True Truth" about this situation that is giving me this Negative Visceral Reaction?

Here are some True Truths to consider:

- Every child born on earth is deserving of love, security and opportunity
- Our bodies are perfectly designed for us, each in its own unique, individual way
- We deserve to be healthy.
- We deserve to be overflowing with abundance in our life
- Everyone deserves love

- Everyone deserves to feel safe
- Everyone deserves all their needs to be met
- There is a Universal Higher Power that loves you and adores you
- Every child deserves to feel happy
- You deserve happiness, joy and wealth
- A good education is not necessary for you to be successful

I could go on and on, but chances are I have listed enough Truths to cause a "Visceral Reaction" in your gut.

Some of these Truths may be easy for you to digest, but there may be some that go against what you have been conditioned to believe. You may have accepted some "false" Truths throughout your life. These false truths will cause you to say NO to the list I just presented to you. "NO!" "Those things cannot be Truth!" Don't be discouraged if your head says things like, "Wait! Everyone deserves EVERYTHING?" "That is all a fairy tale!" "That is not MY reality!" This may remind you of a bunch of political rhetoric that promises everything but has no basis in reality. If that is your reaction; if that is how you feel, don't be disturbed by your inability to accept these Truths. We will tackle them soon enough.

Just "believe" that with whatever is going on in our life, we will "know" when we are back in Alignment with the Truth when we feel our Gut calm down.

You may need to do some digging to find out which Core Beliefs have been adopted and trapped into your Head Brain and caused you to be unable to easily connect to the Visceral messages from your Gut. These Core Beliefs keep our minds from seeing the beauty and possibilities available to us in our lives. If you are someone who is looking for full healing from your limiting thoughts and beliefs that are mastered by playing a Victim or a Villain, wonderful.

My guess is, seeing that you have made it this far in the book - you are truly open to healing and connecting with the True Truth which allows you to stay in a positive Visceral alignment. But how do we get back into the True Truth? I'm so glad you asked. In the next two Vs, we will address the two most powerful Vs in the process; Vulnerable & Vested.

Let's move on to the Fourth V.

Let's Contemplate "Visceral"

Questions About Navigating your Negative Visceral State

- Do I feel Viscerally calm, or disturbed inside?
- Am I being a Victim?
- Am I being a Villain?
- What is the True Truth about the situation which is giving me a Negative Visceral reaction?
- If I cannot find "My Truth" with this situation, what is the Truth on a global human scale?
- Does everyone truly deserve happiness?
- Would I put another person through the same rigorous standards I'm holding myself to?
- If someone I loved felt about themselves the way I feel about myself when Viscerally disturbed – would I want for them to heal?
- What are my thoughts about my worth or value that cause me to have a negative visceral reaction when I listen to them?

- What thoughts about myself cause me to have a calm / aligned Visceral state when I listen to them?

With whatever is going on in our life, we will know we are back in alignment with True Truth when we feel the Visceral Reaction calm down.

7

V4 – VULNERABLE

*As children, we are born completely "Vulnerable." We are open to everything the world has to offer. When a child falls Victim to an adult's Fears, Lies, or judgments- their ability to remain "Vulnerable" can be affected. As an adult, we become the one feeding ourselves truths and non-truths. In my scariest adult moments, I have always been faced with the **choice** of putting up a wall and protecting myself, or the **choice** of opening up and being "Vulnerable" to the situation in its entirety. When I have chosen to be "Vulnerable," I have found that I am actually the strongest and the most present. In other words, I don't miss a single part of the experience.*

Vulnerable - adjective

- Willing to show emotion without closing off to the responses of others
- Open to criticism or experiencing things
- Capable of being physically or emotionally wounded

Synonyms: disarmed, open to, tender, sensitive, breakable, at risk

Oxford Dictionary

If you were to ask me what I most feared as a young adult, one of my top answers would have been the feeling of being "Vulnerable."

Vulnerable is not a word that is met with great excitement in my experience. I can speak first-hand on this subject since I spent so much time being what I perceived to be the Victim of other people's actions. Part of my "survival skills" included shutting down my emotions and hiding them away so no one could identify or get close to them. My goal was to stay as far away from "Vulnerable" as I could get.

In shutting down emotionally, I intentionally took away the power that other people could use to hurt me. In my opinion, being Vulnerable meant being weak and open to damage from other people. I was willing to lose out on any experience so long as I felt safe. I would do anything to avoid emotional or physical pain. It felt lonely at times. I lost people, opportunities for growth, jobs and self-esteem all in the name of "not being weak." I would go back and forth in my willingness to want to open up, then become afraid and shut my feelings down.

I cannot tell you the amount of times I shut down and missed great opportunity for growth which would leave me with a feeling of regret. The ability to stay disconnected from others became harder after I had my children. Or when I lost friends that I could have been closer to, if I had only been willing to risk Vulnerability. As time went on, I experienced situations in my life where I came to realize that being Vulnerable was the only way I was going to get the resolve I was looking for. As I continued to work on myself and become more and more emotionally healthy, I started to desire more connection. After all, I had been on a journey looking for a destination. That destination was felt deep down in a Visceral place. It was being able to clearly be in the moment with the "True Truth." Being Vulnerable was the only way to connect on the deeper level I was desiring to connect on. Being Vulnerable was the only way to take the leaps of faith I needed to change the direction of my life, including my financial situation. I had to be brave enough to fail. So, slowly along time, with every new situation I encountered, I mustered up the courage to be Vulnerable, hoping to avoid losing out on an opportunity or true connectedness with those I cared for.

I hope that you can connect to at least some of the things I talk about in this chapter. My wish for you is to step out of the current flow of life you are currently attached to and to find new experiences through leaps of faith and taking risks. Imagine what your life would look like if you chose to connect deeper to the people you love, apply for jobs you really want, dive in to the hobbies you enjoy. What would your life look and feel like if you allowed people to see you for who you really are? The childlike soul you were born with. What would happen if you chose to put down the mask you choose to wear sometimes and let people really see how wonderful you are? You already know what life feels like at your current level of Vulnerability – whether that be a little bit Vulnerable, or not at all. I challenge you to open up a little more each day to your Authentic Self and let it shine. But to choose to be Vulnerable is to choose to be incredibly brave and strong. The question is this - do you have the strength to be Vulnerable? If you don't think that you do, then the other question is this... "what or whom would you have to lose to finally see the VALUE in being Vulnerable?"

If the thought of allowing people the opportunity to reject or hurt you is too scary, I get it. I have felt that way myself. Being Vulnerable has never been a state that I ever remember wanting to be when I was younger. Vulnerable to me had meant "weak", "stupid", "pathetic." I felt like I had been Vulnerable many times in my life and it never seemed to have paid off.

But I had confused myself about the difference between playing the Victim and choosing to be Vulnerable. I had learned through the years to guard myself heavily from anything that could possibly hurt or harm me. If it scared me or posed any threat at all emotionally, I rejected it or fought violently against it inside.

If you have ever experienced deep emotional pain like I have, I can only imagine that your thoughts would be as strong as mine used to be against making a choice to become Vulnerable.

Being a Victim so many times throughout my youth and into my adult life, I had found myself in situations where I felt I was helplessly Vulnerable.

As a child, I felt that way. I honestly had no choice in the matter but to be Victim to the words and actions of the adults around me. As a child, I was Vulnerable in the sense that I couldn't stop the adults around me from harming me. I was without a voice in the situation. But as an adult, many of these situations where I found myself playing the role of a Victim were those times when I chose to sell out my own happiness for the comfort of others. In other words, I chose to play the Victim.

Choosing to play the Victim is NOT the same as choosing to be Vulnerable.

There have also been unfortunate times where I found myself in situations where, as an adult, I truly was a Victim and could do nothing about it at the time. But, when I could finally do something about it, I did. After it was over, I was presented with the option of deciding what kind of meaning I would give that moment I had experienced. Was there a hidden gift or lesson from my experiences? I chose to embrace the damage and own the experiences I had been given. I chose then to use those stories for the good lessons it offered to those around me.

There were also other times in which I found it hard to move forward from some of these circumstances where I found myself to be in situations where I truly was a Victim. I wanted to move forward but was frozen. I do my best not to fault myself for the moments that I've stayed stuck or found moving forward to be difficult for me. I have found that no matter how stuck I have been, there has always been something I've learned by experiencing each situation in exactly the way I did.

Looking back on my life there, have been many times I have refused to be Vulnerable with a person or situation and didn't see the harm I was doing to myself by keeping myself closed off. But now in revisiting these choices in my mind, I see that there were so many times I could have experienced so much more in life had I been strong and brave enough to be open and "Vulnerable."

I have also taken notice that anytime I have regretted a choice I've made in a situation, the Universe has given me an opportunity to make a different choice in a similar situation. This rings true for my journey to becoming more Vulnerable. Where I have chosen to be closed off and regretted it, I have been given the opportunity to make a different choice in a different situation. Same fear, different scenario.

Let me tell you about two powerful experiences where I chose in the first one, to stay "safe." In the second one, I chose to feel the pain I knew was inevitable and be Vulnerable instead.

When I was in my mid-twenties, I had a friend named Sarah. I was brand new in my journey of recovery and didn't have many friends. Sarah saw me struggling and went out of her way to befriend me. She made it so much easier to face the tough times that early sobriety held for me and allowed me to lean on her day and night.

Sarah came to my house and checked in on me quite often. She took the time out of her life to make sure that I had someone to hang out with instead of going to the bar. She showed up at my house at least 5 times per week just to chat and let me know that she cared, and I was not alone.

One night, Sarah called and said she was on her way over but never made it to my house. I called over and over again that night and continued calling for 3 weeks straight. She was the only real friend I had at the time. I took her unresponsiveness personally and I felt the rejection so deep in my heart. I felt like I was duped, and that she didn't really care about me at all. I fell into the Victim role in my mind, feeling sorry for myself and reprimanding myself for being Vulnerable and letting someone in. I reminded myself that "people don't really care" and that "I knew better than to trust my heart to another person."

I received a phone call late one night from Sarah. I heard her voice on the other end of the line and told her that I was angry. By that time, I had already made the decision that I would close my heart off to Sarah and not let her hurt me again. I beat myself up for being weak and pathetic and letting someone in. I knew better. Didn't I?!

She spoke kindly as I told her how many times I had called her, and how inconsiderate she had been to me. She never got mad or even raised her voice during the conversation. When I was finished talking, Sarah explained to me why she wasn't able to call. On the night she was supposed to come over to my house, Sarah had a seizure and was put into the hospital. In the hospital, she found out that she had a rare type of brain cancer which was extremely aggressive and untreatable due to the nature of how it spreads like fingers throughout the brain. She explained to me that the growth of this type of cancer was rapid and she wasn't expected to live much longer.

I was immediately ashamed, and I was also so scared

and sad for her. She told me that she had worried about me while she was in the hospital and how her parents relayed every message I left on their phone.

I remember the fear that came over me as I hung up the phone; the thoughts of shame and guilt. I thought about how scary the thought of losing her was. I wasn't very emotionally healthy at this stage of my life and I immediately made her situation about myself. I felt the fear and the impending loss which signaled to me that it was now necessary to put up my protection mechanisms and detach. Quickly.

I promised her I would call, but I didn't call. I was so scared of the pain that I believed I would eventually feel from the loss that I just stopped communicating altogether.

I chose to avoid being "Vulnerable" and risking feeling the pain that was sure to come. Instead, I sat and felt sorry for myself as though I was the one who was afflicted with the cancer. I found such a deep and profound self-judgment during that time and feeling sorry for myself was a way out. I went into total denial about Sarah's illness. If I didn't acknowledge it, it didn't exist.

When she passed away, I couldn't bring myself to go to the funeral. Once again, I found a reason to blame somewhere outside myself for my unhappiness and loss. I made the decision that I would blame God. God had dangled a friendship in front of me and then ripped it away, He had set me up for the pain I was feeling.

I felt a sick sense of justification for the rules of "no one gets close" settle in. I talked about how this "so called" Higher Power had "tricked" and "Victimized" me one more time, again.

In truth, The Universe had created a classroom which starred two beautiful young women who were each given unusual situations they weren't prepared to experience; that one would die, and the other would carry the experience on into her future.

Some years later, I was called in to a hospital to go meet with a 14-year-old girl who was struggling with an addiction to pain medication. Since pain medication was where I had started my journey, I felt a true connection to those addicted to pills and felt I could give them a supportive hand and, possibly, help them navigate a way to get out of the addiction successfully.

I went in and met Em. She was just the sweetest human being I had ever met in my life. There was an intoxicating magic about her. She was soft spoken with these large deep insightful brown eyes that trapped your heart when she spoke to you. She was also so very funny and full of personality.

I felt an immediate connection to her. We talked for hours before I got up finally to leave. I gave her my phone number and promised to keep in touch with her and help her in any way I could with her recovery. I was so excited to get to know this young woman and help her.

Upon leaving, I was told by the staff that she had cancer. The minute I heard that word "cancer," I felt the fear come over me instantly. I felt my defenses rise. I decided in my Head Brain that this was not something I wanted to experience again, and no matter how drawn I was to her - it would probably be best for all parties if I stayed distant.

She called me later that night. I immediately started to tell her how busy my life was and then I gave her a phone number to call. I passed her off to one of the girls I sponsored in my 12-step program to help her out and told Em that I would be here if the other girl didn't work out.

I made up some story about how the other girl was younger and she probably would be able to connect with her in an easier way. Viscerally, I felt in my Gut Brain that this was not the right thing to do, but the inner dialogue my Head Brain had created did a good job of quieting that Visceral reaction. I rationalized my decision to make excuses as to why I needed to stay at arm's length. I was feeling the loss of Sarah again in my Heart. That is why I did everything in my power to close off the Vulnerability I felt towards the situation. I still continued to talk to Em, but I didn't want to get too deeply involved lest I get hurt again by another cancer death.

It's funny how the Universe will continually bring the same lesson up over and over again. It is also funny how I can be so completely ignorant of these lessons when they show up. I have learned that when God's will for us to heal is greater than our will for us to stay sick, He finds a way to make sure that happens. His will be done – can't stop the Universe from continuing! No matter how or what you or I believe, this is True Truth in action.

I had no idea that this was a lesson for healing that I was being presented with because I was too preoccupied with my negative thoughts that this was just another situation where I was going to eventually get hurt again. Still blaming God, all I thought about was that I had heard it said too many times before, "If you want to make God laugh - tell him your plans."

Em wasn't aware of it at the time, but she was to be my greatest teacher. For me, my healing and embracing of Vulnerability came through this young, headstrong, amazing young woman in spite of my own plans.

This crazy little teenager felt a connection with me and never let me alone. Ever. I smile so big right now remembering how afraid I was of her Vulnerability and eagerness to live life and experience everything her heart desired. Every day she would call. Every 12 Step meeting I would go to; she would be there. Every time we talked, she would constantly tell me that I needed to be her sponsor.

Eventually, I ended up saying yes to sponsoring her. It was one of the best risks I have ever taken. We became inseparable, and years later she would ask me to take the role of being her Godmother, which I gladly and proudly accepted.

As the years went by, I learned to be Vulnerable with the help of Emily. She offered me the opportunity to be Vulnerable in a way that felt quite safe even though it was still very uncomfortable for me to do.

I did my best to show up for the most part, but when I would think about the fact that someday I would lose her, I would randomly pull away. It was so difficult.

I fell in love with her as though we were family. At times, I just limped through my fear of her abandoning me, even though the screaming in my head to pull away as she got closer and closer to me became incredibly deafening.

I let her down over and over again because of my fears. She would have important occasions that she asked me to attend and I would conveniently become "too ill" to show up. I never lied to her. I didn't make up the fact I got sick, but I would always get sick when it was important for me to be well. The body will do that for the Head Brain. It will make us sick right at the most

Vulnerable moments. Thank God she loved me so much. I was always letting her down and she was always saying she forgave me.

Over the next decade, she would continue on by remaining on a low dose of chemo, but the cancer stayed and reared its ugly head quite regularly. It truly scared me. The closer we got, the more I wanted to run.

Over the years of her growth and my own growth, I had continued to do enough self-work to communicate and be Vulnerable in a way that let her know exactly where my shortcomings and fears lay. I could be honest with her and tell her the True Truth Vulnerably, saying exactly what I was experiencing as far as the fears of losing her went. But she continued to tell me, "WELL, I NEED YOU SO GET OVER IT."

Our relationship had gifted me with a powerful opportunity and ability to embrace Vulnerability in a way that was brand new to me. I was forced to learn how to use my Vulnerability as a pathway to find a new level of connectedness to another human being which most people never get to experience. I got to use Vulnerability as a tool for embracing the True Truth. Finally, being able to discover the true nature of the limiting inner dialogue that was really going on in my head when things got scary.

This breakthrough never would have happened had I not had Em or Sarah to guide me there.

About 10 years later into our friendship, I was so happy to have Em tell me that a bone marrow donor had matched with her and that she was going to have a transplant and beat the cancer for good.

I was so overjoyed to hear this news. Thoughts of gratitude and prayers filled with thanks flew out of my heart to my Higher Power! Finally, I felt God was on my side!

She had the bone marrow transplant and was free of cancer for the first time since she was 7 years old. Aside from my children being born, and the marriage to my husband, I had never felt that much happiness in my whole life. Unfortunately, that happiness lasted less than a year.

I got the news that cancer had come back in another form. Em had a seizure and when they performed tests in the hospital, they found cancer in her brain this time. She was told that she would soon die. I had never wanted to shut down or run away more than I wanted to when I heard this news. But I was in too deep. As her Godmother, I would do anything she asked. I loved her so much I would never abandon her.

She asked me to come take shifts at the hospital with her in her room. I would stay up at night with her in her bed; laying there for hours talking about everything we could think of. Often the conversations turned serious, and it was almost unbearable.

As her cancer progressed - she eventually developed a brain tumor and went blind. By this time, I had become completely comfortable with being Vulnerable with her. We spoke of everything from music to God and everything in between. She was the safest human I knew. She was the closest friend I ever had.

During one of our conversations after she had gone blind, I asked her, "So- if everything in this world happens for a reason, why do you think you went blind?" Her answer floored me. She said something along the lines of "Mama, you know I used to think it mattered how much fat I had on my stomach, or what my hair looked like, or what my make-up looked like - but it took me going blind to see anything at all. The only thing that matters is Love."

That moment changed me forever. They were the wisest words any human had ever said to me. It was a moment in my life I will never forget. As her own mother lay there in the room with us sleeping, I couldn't help but be so happy for her to have enjoyed being a mother to such an insightful and incredible child, and I also ached for her and her husband's eventual loss of such a young angel.

Here I was a teacher of Spirituality and Empowerment, and yet - that little girl taught me more about Spirituality and Empowerment than anyone I had ever met. She taught me how to be Vulnerable with a strength I never thought possible.

I struggled still with my own values when it came to being her friend. My Head would have so many thoughts running through it about how much I didn't deserve to have her love. I would recount all the times I had let her down.

Even though I felt so lucky to be her "earth angel," as she called me - my heart still wanted to be protected from this pain. I was afraid of the imminent loss, but in my Gut, a deep Visceral reaction kept reminding me that I had to stay connected. I knew I would feel a regret I would never forgive myself for if I chose to run away.

I sat in reflection as my three Brains were fighting with each other. My Head Brain was saying "RUN!" My Heart Brain was saying "Protect us from the pain that will come from this loss!" And my Gut was sending me the message to, "Stay the course! It may hurt but it is the right thing to do and you will be glad you did!"

It was so scary, but I knew it was the only way to approach this situation. I had already experienced losing a friend to cancer and not engaging. I was not going to play the Villain again with Em by repeating and feeling those feelings I had experienced with Sarah.

With all my heart I sank vulnerably into my relationship with Em and EVERYTHING it had to offer; the love, the pain, the connection and the eventual loss. When my Head and my Heart would pipe up, I would refer to my Visceral Vibration and remember the True Truth which was, "I loved this girl, I am going to lose this girl, and I want to experience every moment that I can with her." My Visceral Reaction calmed when I remembered the Truth and embraced it. I am SO GLAD I did. Until her, I never knew what true friendship was.

I cannot imagine the void that would remain if I had lost out on the experience and gift it was to be in her presence. She was my teacher and I was hers.

I remember telling her once that I used to think that I was there to help save her, but I came to realize that she was there to save me. She nodded to me and said, "Yep, I think you're right." She gave me the gift of being able to embrace true Vulnerability and feel the strength the act of being Vulnerable truly brings.

It takes true strength to show up willing to be Vulnerable.

I think that embracing Vulnerability, for some of my students, is the most powerful of all the Five V's for it allows for True and Unconditional love to have a voice. It allows for experiences to happen that otherwise would be impossible. But even though the power is felt on a deep level, it can also be the scariest V for some to embrace.

When people hear me tell them that Vulnerable is the 4th V, often I get a variety of eye rolls, grunts and groans. I've had people get angry (scared) and ask me how I could POSSIBLY ask them to now open themselves up after we've so clearly demonstrated how they have been Victimized and hurt. I have already asked them to acknowledge how they have become their own Villain. How could I ask them now to take such a position of weakness?!

I simply reply with this: Once we put into practice and it becomes a routine response, it comes to the fore and becomes effortless. Thus, it takes less strength and energy to go out in this world with an open heart and risk failure or rejection than it took to remain guarded, aggressive, detached or invisible. How many people truly got to know the real you while you were so busy playing the Victim or the Villain?

You have come this far, and I promise it is not for nothing. I will give you all the tools you will need in these Five V's, but you will need to be the one to make the choice to be strong enough to be Vulnerably "You." You have the tools and opportunity to move on to the 5th V and embrace your Authentic Self.

I can't express to you strongly enough the fact that if I hadn't decided to embrace Vulnerability, I would have squandered away numerous relationships, experiences and opportunities which were available to me to experience.

A life without Vulnerability is a missed opportunity for true connectedness and hinders us from experiencing a full and complete life.

Vulnerability involves taking a risk that opens up our lives for more love, more happiness, more success, more experience and more "life." The same goes for the less serious things.

Career, adventure, love, spirituality - all of it.... without risking being Vulnerable, all that we are left with is the mundane and the ordinary, the misconceived "safe" life which leads to regret in the end.

There are people who have embraced a life of sitting and waiting. They wake up in the morning, get ready for work, sit on a bus, sit in traffic, sit on the train only to arrive at work where they sit at a desk, sit and wait until the work day is over, only to sit in traffic on the way home where they sit in front of the tv and wait until it's time to go to bed where they can wake up and do it all over again.

In going through the Visceral Awareness mentioned in

the chapter before this, we ask ourselves if we feel that this is the way our lives are supposed to be? Are we satisfied with where our lives are? When we think of those we love, are we satisfied with our Visceral Reaction to them? How many relationships can be healed, or become even stronger if we decide to be brave enough to be Vulnerable with ourselves and others?

If we have hurts or damaged relationships hanging in the back of our heart, we have the chance to make things right by embracing "Vulnerability." If we yearn for a career or life where we will feel satisfied and alive, we have the chance to create that now by embracing "Vulnerability."

Yes, we may need to get Vulnerable and put ourselves out there and risk success. Maybe risk failing as well. Yes, risking growth by being Vulnerable to old hurts and new or unexperienced situations is scary. But even more scary than that is the thought of possibly living an entire life without ever truly being Vulnerable and not experiencing everything that is available for us to experience.

We are all meant to flourish, not be a cookie cutter of society's idea of having a "successful" and "productive" existence. I don't believe anyone is born with a desire to be mundane or ordinary. Those things are taught to us out of fear. We are conditioned to want those things. We call it "security." I believe every human is born with the desire to be adventurous and explore life. In order to accomplish this end, we must remain Vulnerable and be willing to risk failure. Being truly Vulnerable allows for a deeper connection and greater growth in all things we choose to experience.

We have learned a lot about how we were born with pure potential. We have been hurt or scared and in turn have shut down or adopted other people's rules and opinions only to become a masked version of ourselves.

But what now comes is the real question of, "Who are we, really?"

Which brings us to our final V... Vested.

Questions About Your Vulnerability

Questions to ask yourself about your own Vulnerability.

- In what areas of your life are you "Playing it Safe" and avoiding Vulnerability?

- What would happen if you opened yourself up for risk by showing your true self off or opening up to those around you?

- If this is scary, what little things could you do right now to be brave and Vulnerable in your life?

- What relationships could you heal now by opening up to the full experience of what those relationships have to offer?

8

V5 - VESTED

There is a difference between being "invested" and "vested" in a belief or an idea. Being "Vested" in the True Truth about ourselves and others is a continual process. One's version of the "Truth" is open to their interpretation and point of view. The "Vested Truth," or the "True Truth" can neither be shaken or refuted - it is the same "Truth" no matter what angle of perception you look at it from. When we are "Vested," we will not fall prey to the opinions or confusion of others.

Vested -Adjective

- Fully and unconditionally guaranteed as a legal right, benefit or privilege.
- Secured in the possession of or assigned to a person
- Having the absolute right to or authority to own without risk of loss
- Synonyms: unconditional, secure, stable, unshakable, rooted, permanent

Oxford Dictionary

Ah. Vested. The final "V". Also, the most important one of all. Being Vested means living in "The True Truth." A truth that cannot be shaken or taken from you. The word Vested is commonly used as a describer for how much of something is completely held or owned by a person. Vested: If something you own is Vested, that means it is held completely, permanently and inalienably for you and it cannot be taken away from you, but you can choose to give it away if you want.

I OWN AND AM VESTED IN MY OWN TRUE TRUTH - NOT YOURS OR ANYONE ELSES... MINE ALONE.

My Vested Truth cannot be changed by someone else.

We are all worthy of happiness. If I am confused about my worthiness, this means I am only "invested" in the idea that I am not worthy of happiness. It is a false truth that can be changed and healed by my own investigation or other people's words. When I am "Vested" in the True Fact that all of us are worthy of happiness, it cannot be challenged or changed by other's opinions.

Believe me, many have tried to give me every reason why some people deserve happiness, and others don't.

FRANKI OLINGER

They cannot convince me because I am "Vested" in the "True Truth" concerning this matter.

There was a time when I was sure this was true for others, but I wasn't sure if it was true for me. I have flip-flopped with the belief of deserved happiness over the years numerous times.

One person would tell me I was worthless, and no one is automatically deserving of being "happy." This immediately affected me when I heard these words and I had chosen to believe that it was true.

Then another person would come along and tell me that I "absolutely had a right to be happy and that everyone deserves happiness" and I would perk up again.

I would tell the next person who told me that I was worthless, and no one actually "deserves" to be happy, that I had been told that **everyone** deserves happiness.

That person would tell me that I was not living in reality and should stop letting that other person "blow sunshine up my a**."

This cycle would go on and on with many different players with many different beliefs, in many different

203

scenarios. I was always "invested" in the idea of these Truths that felt so good to believe, but the problem was that I was never really "Vested" in those Truths because they never really came from **me**. This is where the need for being Vested in the True Truth, MY TRUTH comes in. If I am living my life from the viewpoint that "other people know the truth more than I do," then depending on the person- and how much power I give their opinion, I will always be adopting and living someone else's Truth.

Being part of the present human race, I am naturally drawn to the idea of being respected or accepted by others. Sometimes the desire to be liked or respected have worked against me.

Before I became brave enough to be "Vested" in who I really am, I spent many years adjusting my likes, personality and desires to match what I felt would gain me the most acceptance. I pretended I wasn't mad, pretended I was happy, pretended I was mad, pretended I liked a particular band or artist, even pretended I didn't like someone based on the opinions of those I surrounded myself with. I pretended whatever I needed to pretend to be accepted.

Boy, that was a lot of pretending! I would always try to figure out who I "should" or "shouldn't" be, based on the present company I was with.

I was never really Authentic or Vested in my own Truth because it was more important to be liked, or safe, or accepted. I spent a lot of time figuring out who I "should" or "shouldn't" be, what I "should" or "shouldn't" like and what I "should" or "shouldn't" think or feel. I changed my words to please others or to please the voice of my ego, my Head Brain's demands.

I would like to talk a moment about those two words, "should and shouldn't" at this time. I call them "Judgment" words. As a person who is interested only in the "Vested Truths" I hold for myself, these are two words that I do my best to avoid entertaining in my Head Brain today.

I have experienced the power of the "should" or "shouldn't" thoughts many times over the years.

I remember having a conversation with a friend about 2 years after the death of my ex and I was expressing the fact that I still was very sad and affected by it. I needed to talk to someone about it.

She became very cold and told me that it had been enough years since that had happened and that I "should" be "over it" by now. I remember feeling shame and embarrassment that I was still grieving and told her that she was right. I "should" be over it by now. I stuffed it inside and pretended I was totally fine with it after that.

But the truth is that I wasn't fine with it, at all. I wasn't over it. And I was still grieving terribly. I didn't mention it again for years after that. I didn't go see a therapist because of her words which became my inner words. "It's been long enough, I should be over it." I became invested in the thought that there was something wrong with me for still grieving this many years later. I let her give me her truth and I owned it as THE TRUTH. I took on someone else's truth and decided that I "should" put a judgment in my heart towards my grieving process. I was angry at myself for not grieving the right way. I rejected my feelings and beat myself up in my head for being so "weak" and "pathetic." I hid that part of myself in fear of being rejected or judged on the outside by anyone for many years. Instead I drank and pretended everything was great.

In our process of becoming our Authentic Vested Self, those words "should and shouldn't" are opposing to the process. Maybe I "shouldn't" have been affected by the death after two years. But I was. So, in being Vested and Authentic, I needed to find and own exactly what the True Truth was. I had to decide on MY truth, and I had to be Vested for it to take hold, even if the Truth was contrary to another person's truth.

In my healing, I cannot process something if I pretend it doesn't exist. Really! I cannot heal a wound which I pretend isn't there. So, today I own my Truth as my own, regardless of what anyone else's Truth is. The truth is that it took me over two decades to process and come to a Vested place of healing with that death and that is okay.

Being authentic and Vested in my True Truth is a process which takes time. I have found that is also an ever-changing metamorphosis. It changes as I go along.

If I am only "invested" in a Truth today, it may easily be changed tomorrow. Remember what I told you about "invested" and "Vested"? If I am confused or unsure about something, I am only "invested." If I am "Vested," it cannot be taken away.

If it is a Truth that can be changed, it is a Truth that you are only "invested" in. It takes some self-examination on your part into your so-called "Truths and Opinions" to really know whether or not it is a "Vested Truth" or just an "invested truth."

For example: When I started my own personal process of finding my "Vested Truths, I decided to start with silly things such as food preferences. I started with the letter A.

I searched my palate for foods I hated, and Artichoke was one that I had always told others that I hated. But I couldn't call to mind trying them except for once when I was a child. I had professed my disgust with them numerous times since I was a child. So, I decided to try an artichoke. I looked up how to make an artichoke and I cooked it and ate it. It was delicious.

I laughed at the fact I was so SURE that I thought they were gross. It was love at first bite. I've been eating artichokes ever since. This may seem like a silly example but think about it. How many things are you sure that you like or don't like, but haven't had any experience (or maybe had one bad experience) with?

What if you went back through all of your "Truths" and found that you liked that band that your best friend in high school hated? You've been missing out on the joy of that music for a long time now. Start playing investigator when your opinions come up and ask yourself why those opinions are so true for you.

One of my favorite questions to ask a client when I start working with them is "Who are you, really?" It's a simple question which seems like it would be easy to answer right away. I ask them to give me an "I Am" Statement. But I ask them to take a few minutes before they answer. I suggest they really sit with their thoughts and allow those thoughts to resonate "Viscerally" throughout their body. I tell them to ask themselves if what they are about to say is their Truth, or someone else's Truth. I ask them if they are sure that it is their Truth. I ask them to tell me why they know it to be the Truth. What is their evidence?

Sometimes when they tell me an answer and it hits a Visceral nerve in me, I ask them if their answer is what they truly know to be accurate. Are they looking to give me the "right" answer or the answer that I am looking for?

THE FIVE V's – A GUIDE TO EMPOWERMENT & HAPPINESS

Other times when I ask the question of "Who are you," to a client or a student, they are unable to go much deeper beyond the surface than, "I am a Mom," or "I am an accountant," or "I am an artist."

When answering this question, we also have to take into consideration that our answer may change from moment to moment. "I am a patient person" may change when they are late for an important occasion. A person who identifies with being "creative" may find that they do not identify with that label first thing in the morning. They may only be creative at nighttime. If this is the case, then they have the opportunity to get to the True Truth, The Authentic Vested Self. Again, it takes a bit of self-examination.

Some people have been trained by their parents, peers or society to identify as things like "Christian, Buddhist, Agnostic, successful, loser, winner, gifted, etc." But again. this is not the answer to the question of "Who are you?" If you are anything like me, it took some time and effort to really connect with the Truth about who and what I really am.

Being fully Vested in your Personal Truth is a freedom that can only be owned and experienced in full by yourself. You are the only one who is identifying with your "I Am" statement.

Being Vested is an intimate and sacred pact you have with yourself. Allowing another person to define you will only give an illusion of Truth about your "I Am" statements. If you ask twenty different people to write down who they "think" you are, you may get a lot of Truths, but I would bet that they tend to differ depending on who you ask. Ask your best friend and your worst enemy to define you. You will most likely get two very differing descriptions but only you will be able to feel Viscerally what the "True Truth" is.

Try on an outfit some time and ask five different people whether or not they like that outfit. You, the person wearing the clothing as well as the outfit you are asking about will not change, but the opinions will vary from person to person and they will be different depending on the personal preference and personality of each person giving their opinion.

So, in reality, they are not defining your choice in outfits - or yourself - but it may feel that way. The only one who knows the True Truth is you. You will need to ask yourself a better set of questions. Do I like this outfit?

Why did I choose it? What meaning does this outfit give to me about me?

When we apply questions like these to all aspects of our life, we will begin to be able to figure out whether we are truly "Vested" in our Truths, or just "invested" in them.

Many people confuse "Vested" with "InVested." There is a BIG DIFFERENCE between the two if you take the time to look at them. When someone invests in something, (usually something of value like a stock, a property, an idea or even a relationship) any of these things can be lost at any time through circumstances such as an accident, bad judgment, luck of the draw or any other reason. With an investment, you risk losing this thing to another or even no one.

But if you are FULLY "Vested" in an idea or situation, your Truth cannot be taken from you for any reason. You can choose to give it away, but it cannot be taken. Your empowerment is your right and your choice.

This is the part where I implore you to go back through all of the previous Vs and become very honest with who you really are:

- Investigate where you have been conditioned and Victimized by yourself or others.

- Where have you been the Villain in your own life and others?

- What is the Visceral reaction you feel when you think about these people, places or moments in time that you were Conditioned, Victimized or played the Villain?

- Identify where your dreams were replaced with other people's dreams, rules and judgment.

FIND THE LIES.

Feel your Visceral reactions as you explore each of your present circumstances with all three of your Brains (Your Head, Your Heart, and Your Gut).

What Truth causes the Visceral reaction to become calm? Sometimes it takes a lot to admit to the True Truth about who we really are and what we really think or believe. Our own judgments about "labels and types of people" may leave us fighting against admitting certain aspects about ourselves which are true.

Take me for example. I have been called a "control freak" my whole life. It has never been something I particularly enjoyed being called. It has actually angered me whenever someone would have the audacity to say those rude words to me. It immediately gave me a violent and disturbed Visceral reaction inside.

I remember, in particular, the very last time I truly battled against the thought of identifying as a control freak.

I had a roommate who owned this cute little dog named "Villain" (ironic, isn't it?) and this cute little dog made use of my bed as a place to relieve himself one night (unbeknownst to me) while I was sleeping. I literally laid there unaware that night and, at some point in time, rolled over in my sleep to wake up covered in dog shit. No lie. What a way to wake up!

I went to my roommate and demanded she clean it up and apologize to me.

In our "discussion" of the situation, she pointed out how I was a total control freak and our friendship instantly took a hiatus. I was sure it was her fault; she was sure I was just being a controlling bitch.

In seething over the audacity for her to have called me a control freak, I went over every reason why not only was she out of line, but she was also quite wrong! I went over ways in my head to force her to see the error of her ways and admit I was in the right and she was in the wrong.

This friend of mine, a friend of many years, moved out of my house and I stewed in anger, also sadness that this had gone so far. I wondered what she was telling other people about me. I stopped talking to mutual friends in the fear that they would be on her side. In the fear that she had told them I was the control freak and she was in the right.

I would see her in public and every time I would fight the urge to walk up and tell her how I AM NOT A CONTROL FREAK and what about the dog shitting in my bed? Where's my apology?! How is this mine and not your dog's fault?

I went to my husband and asked him, "Can you believe that instead of admitting she was wrong and cleaning it up, she called me a control freak?!" I could see the look in my husband's eyes, as he fought against the voices in his head telling him to stay quiet, as he blurted out, "Well, honey, you kind of are a control freak... a little."

Goddamnit! That was it, he was on her side now?!

I went to my daughter, "Can you believe she called ME a control freak?!"

Oh shit... there was that look again. "Well, Mom, you can be a little controlling sometimes... a lot of the ti... sometimes."

Screw her... they were all in on it together. I can't see how they don't see that the dog is the problem! How can they not see that her inability to apologize is the problem? HOW DID THIS TURN IN TO ME BEING A CONTROL FREAK?! My Visceral reaction to this situation was through the roof!

I plotted on how I was going to convince these other people that I am not a control freak! I must find a way to control this situ.......... and then it dawned on me, oh my God. My evidence of the Truth was slapping me in the face. There it was, the True Truth.

I realized, then and there, that I went first to the place of deciding that I was a Victim. I then reacted and became the Villain. As I recognized these Truths about the situation, my Visceral Reaction was shaken to the point that I couldn't ignore the facts...

I WAS A TOTAL CONTROL FREAK

I had lied to myself to save myself from admitting the True Truth which was gnawing inside me in the form of a Visceral hurricane. Even though it was true that I did my best to show up as a tender, supporting, loving and nurturing person to everyone I encountered, it didn't change the fact that when I am upset, when I know I am right, or feel wronged - I was a control freak.

That's the truth, I thought. I am upset because I am living a lie. The second I said it out loud, the Visceral reaction went away.

I went to my husband and I was so excited to tell him that I was a control freak, that I had embraced this Truth and I was okay to know and admit that! And in admitting that, I felt a freedom from that Visceral disturbance inside that I had never felt before that moment. My whole body relaxed - a lot.

My friend and I laugh about it today - and ironically enough, last weekend she asked me for advice about what to do about a family member whose dog had just jumped up on her brand-new car and scratched the side of it. She was upset that her family member didn't apologize for her dog's behavior and we laughed as I reiterated our story to her about this one time I had this roommate that had a dog who took a dump in my bed.

My point is this; we have to learn to admit the truth about ourselves... The Truth shall set us free. Unless we admit we are drowning - we have no reason to ask for a life raft and will continue to sink.

How much time, energy and effort goes into denying things that could be empowering places to heal, but we don't want to admit to ourselves these traits exist? We have to get to our True Truth one way or another.

Going even further in admitting I had the character defect of being a control freak, I also dove further and found a place where my controlling behaviors could be healed and act as an asset.

Let me explain. The one positive perk to having a "control freak" around is that when they are moving towards the direction of Truth and Love - they become wonderful leaders. So, the True Truth is that I have the ability to be a wonderful leader, but when I am working out of fear or believing a lie about a person, place or situation - I can choose to show up as a "Control Freak."

I Victimize others by taking away their voice, or their right to make mistakes or, simply, be wrong about something.

More amazing than this is the fact that once we admit the truth about ourselves, those things which may be seen as less than favorable traits, can be healed and used in a proper way. In learning I was a control freak, I learned where I was causing separation between myself and other people in my life.

Also, in healing the part of me that felt like it needed to control everything and everyone around me, my control turned into leading those who would take my hand and heal. Instead of controlling others, I became a better teacher and coach. I learned to help others during a time when they couldn't or wouldn't make a move for themselves. I was brave enough to help them navigate without fear and keep moving towards the solution to their problems.

Owning the good, bad and indifferent is getting to the True Truth in a way that is freeing and immovable. It is becoming Vested.

It is important that you also own the good as well. After

all, we are looking for only the Truth about ourselves. Without the Truth, there is only a story of what we think it is. Stories can be challenged. Vested Truths cannot be changed by anyone else - but they can be changed by you. If you find that the Vested Truth you believe about yourself is an error, you can find the deeper Truth and embrace that. Again, this can only be done by you alone.

Like my "controlling" behavior. I see it two-fold. I am a control freak when I am not doing well, and I am a good leader when I am well. They are the same thing - but they react differently depending on where I am at in my emotional well-being. I have learned to recognize where I am with this by my Visceral Reaction inside. Always, the "Control Freak" gives me a negative Visceral Reaction whereas the "Good Leader" tends to Viscerally feel "filled with purpose and aligned with those who I am interacting with."

Take the time to really connect with who you really are. One question that I haven't asked you is this: If you had never been exposed to the Victimization you were exposed to as a kid - who would you be today? What might you be like?

Ask your friends or someone you trust to write 10

positive things about you and 5 character flaws that you could work on (be brave and don't argue with what they write).

While reviewing their answers, most importantly - PAY ATTENTION TO YOUR VISCERAL REACTIONS. When you are having a negative Visceral reaction - ask yourself:

"Am I being a Victim - or a Villain when I am considering these things my friend has said I could work on?" Then ask yourself, "What is the True Truth about myself?" and finally "What do I deserve in life?"

WHO IS YOUR VESTED SELF? You will find the answer when you find the True Truth that feels Viscerally settled in your soul.

Whenever a client has a problem coming up with their Vested Truths and they are questioning their Rights and Value, I tell them - "Let's just start from the beginning."

Remember when I told you earlier to line every baby up in the world and tell me which ones didn't deserve this or that? Well, I want you to be one of those babies in your own mind and then ponder each of the below truths.

Every human being deserves the following:

- Happiness

- Joy

- Abundance

- Success

- Adventure

- Freedom to express themselves

- Food

- Air

- Clean Water

- Friendship

- True Love

- Riches

- Opportunity

- Travel

➢ Spirituality

➢ Connectedness

➢ God

➢ Sleeping in

➢ Alone time

➢ Praise

➢ Peace

➢ And whatever else their heart desires.

Every baby was born:

➢ Perfect

➢ Happy

➢ Lovable

➢ Honest

➢ Free

➤   Without Judgment of self

➤   Without Judgment of others

➤   Without fear of adventure

➤   Innocent

➤   Curious

If there is something on the list that you can't resolve yourself to believe someone "deserves"... then ask yourself, "Is there something on this list you would say a baby doesn't deserve?"

If you believe there is anything here that should not be a given right at birth and throughout life, at what point do you believe a person should lose the right to any of these things?

Really, think about it – Every person walking around on this earth deserves everything on this list. No one has the right to deprive their fellow human of these things. In essence, I consider this a **Human's Bill of Rights.**

Once you have begun to find your Vested self, you will

feel the Visceral alignment and peace inside start to happen almost immediately. Our goal is to step out of the lies and confusion and find ourselves in our own True Truth.

The True Truth is used in healing our wounds inside, or the relationship wounds in others by seeing the True Truth and **being Vested** in our own Truth.

Take that adult who abused me as a child. I spent years hating him for what he did to me. I felt he had robbed me of my innocence. He had ruined my ability to trust others. I blamed him for my unhappiness. While I was still a child, this held truth. But as an adult, making my own decisions and choosing my own fate - how could I be empowered and still be blaming someone else for my choices? He was no longer standing there forcing me to do something I didn't want to do; I was the only one there. So, the True Truth was that I was in charge of my own happiness and I chose to sabotage my life and blame him for it.

If I look for the True Truth in him, I have to take into account his upbringing, which I was told included abuse as well. Did that man, as a child, deserve to be abused? Absolutely not. Do I think that had he never been wounded and twisted up by the adults around him, would he have grown up to feel the need to abuse little girls? I doubt it. As a child, that man deserved happiness, joy and love. He deserved to be taught how to handle his feelings and impulses in a healthy way. He learned abuse and violence from those around him. No child deserves that.

Also, if this human had every bit of joy he Divinely was born to receive, he probably wouldn't have had a desire to take it from others in a way that damaged them.

It's interesting, I spoke to that man on the phone quite by accident about 18 months after I got in recovery. I called my Dad's home, and he happened to be there. The moment he answered my Dad's phone, I felt the Visceral Reaction overtake my whole body. I asked him why he was there. He told me he was homeless at the time and had no other place to go, and my dad had let him stay there. Oh boy did the anger take over at that moment. Anger towards him, anger towards my Dad. I asked to speak to my Dad. I was told that my Dad was out with my stepmother and so I promptly hung up on him.

It didn't take long for my Head Brain to kick in with the opinions and the venom it had for that man. And now for my Dad. How could my Dad open his space up to that man after what that man had done to me?! I felt again betrayed and my self-worth felt like it lowered just that much more.

My Vested truth started to take over. I am worthy of love, I am worthy of safety, I am worthy of happiness and joy. I started listening to those True Truths and I felt the Visceral reaction start to subside. But why hadn't it totally subsided? What lie was still continuing underneath my thoughts? I searched and searched and then it hit me. The True Truth about this man was what I was missing. I thought of myself as a baby. If I deserved to be forgiven and happy and all of these freeing things, then I had to look at this man as a baby as well. Didn't he deserve to be forgiven, happy and all the other things that came along with our Divine Human Rights? Yes, he did.

If he was currently homeless and not doing well, wasn't there something preventing him from being happy? Could he be feeling the after-effects of having Victimized someone else?

Would I tell any other person who came to me for help with their inner dialogue that they deserved to suffer over and over again for their past wrongs? Or would I tell them that it's time to forgive?

If I was Vested in the fact that I was a good person, willing to forgive and let things go, then here was my one chance to prove it to myself.

I picked up the phone and dialed the number again. He answered and I proceeded to tell him that I knew what he did to me, and he knew what he did to me. I told him that it didn't matter what anyone else believed because we both knew the truth of what he had done. I told him that I was no longer interested in being mad at him and that I forgave him, and if there was any part of himself that was unable to forgive himself - he should let that go now. There was a moment of silence followed by sobbing on his end of the phone. He told me how heavy all of these years have weighed on his heart and how sorry he was for having done all of that to me. He told me I didn't deserve that; I was a little kid. He also told me that he had waited for years to hear me say something to him. I repeated that I forgave him, and I told him that my life was pretty good now and that he shouldn't worry.

He thanked me again through his tears and I told him I

had to go now, and I hung up.

The disturbing Visceral feeling in my body was gone. I felt the freedom of forgiveness in my heart and I was able to move on from that situation freely.

I called my Dad later that night about the fact that he had let that man in to his home and I questioned him on why he would do that. My Dad said because he felt sorry for him and that he couldn't bring himself to leave that man out in the cold. My dad seemed confused as to why I was so disturbed about him being there. I said, "Because of what he did to me as a kid!" It was that moment that I found out that he had never known about it.

Finding out this truth helped me to heal so many other things inside in an instant. My Dad never talked to me about it because he had never even known it had happened. I gained so much in the forgiveness of that whole situation.

I also gained another Vested Truth which today, cannot be shaken no matter the evidence against it. I am certain that when we forgive, we free ourselves from the attachment to suffering. Once we are free from the suffering part of a situation, we are free from the anger as well. These are True Truths which cannot be shaken or changed no matter how much someone tells me I'm wrong.

Now let's talk about my Mother. I was trapped for years in resentment over her choice to let me go live with another family after I told on that man who abused me. I decided that I was not worthy of love, or protection, or security... add on a plethora of other false truths I adopted.

I didn't speak to my mother after I got into recovery for over a decade. I had run in to her at a family function and called her on Mother's Day once. But for the most part, I couldn't get over my resentment towards her. Or should I say, I refused to.

In 12 Step programs we work through steps. I was a little over 12 Years sober at the time of this particular story and I was currently back on my 8th step. The 8th and 9th steps go hand in hand with each other.

Step 8 when completed says:

"Made a list of all people we had harmed and became willing to make amends to them all."

My sponsor referred to my 4th Step which held all of my resentments against other people and also said where we were accountable to our part in these resentments. My Mother's name was on this list and so she pointed out that if her name was on there, I had some amends to be made to her. I didn't like this idea at all, even though I knew she was right. I told her that no matter what she said, there was no part of me that was interested in talking to my Mom. I was just too angry. So, she prescribed a period of one month to pray for my mother to have all the happiness, joy and love I would want for myself. She also told me that if I missed one day, I would have to start the 30 days over again. I agreed that I would be willing to say those words because my Gut knew she was right, but my Head didn't agree with her.

I prayed that prayer for 30 days straight. At the end of the 30 days, my Sponsor asked me where my head was with it. I told her I was still angry, but I had come to the Truth that she deserved these things and that I wanted her to be happy. I also realized that we were both two adult women and what I was angry about was that my Mother didn't live up to what I thought a Mother should be. I struggled with the fact that I could forgive others for doing such horrible things, but I was having trouble forgiving her for what I felt she had done to me. I told my sponsor I wasn't ready or willing to make the amends yet, but I would keep on praying.

That 30 days of prayer turned in to 9 months of praying every single day until a small miracle of healing happened. I was sitting there in my living room with my husband when my phone got a text message that said; "I think we should love each other again." I read the text out load and I asked my husband what area code 702 was. He told me it was Las Vegas. I shook my head and wondered what ex-boyfriend had gotten my phone number. I put the phone down and I ignored the text.

A few minutes later I got another text that said, "It's your Mom." My body immediately got a strong Visceral reaction which felt like panic and fear. I put the phone down again.

My husband looked at me with those sweet eyes and asked me, "Aren't you going to answer her?" I told him that I didn't know what to say. He simply replied, just tell her the truth.

Another text came in from her asking if she could call. I told her the truth which was that I didn't want to talk to her because I didn't like the way I felt about "myself" when I talked to her.

She then responded, asking that I give her 60 seconds to talk and all I had to do was listen. If I didn't like what I heard, I could hang up.

I said okay and she immediately called. I prayed before I picked up the phone and then I answered. Within 60 seconds my heart melted. My mother called me and told me the truth about me. About what my worth truly was and she talked about her part in my life today. She explained that she watched me on social media, she watched me start to flourish and then crash and burn in my career. She told me she felt that she was partly responsible for how I was acting in my life today. She told me about the lies I believed about myself because of the things I had gone through as a child. She told me the True Truth, and the Visceral reaction went away. I felt calm and healed.

We continued to speak in truth during that conversation. She told me she wanted me in her life again. I wanted that too. But I honestly didn't know how to do that. I told her that I wanted to get to know her as another adult woman, not try to get a mother back. We agreed to speak once a week. I also told her about the book The Four Agreements by Don Miguel Ruiz and told her it was very healing for me, and if she read it, we could probably have a place we could safely communicate from.

It's been over 10 years since that conversation took place and, in that time, I have gotten my Mom back. I have made my amends for where I have hurt her and she has explained to me how a young mother, finding out that her daughter has been abused under her nose thinks and reacts.

I understand today that sending me away was the only thing she could think of to get me out of harm's way immediately. She also told me she would do it again. Because it took me out of harm's way and into safety.

What felt like abandonment and betrayal was actually protection and support. I was just too young to understand that. But as an adult woman, I could feel the truth in her words. Having given away a child for the same purposes in my own life, I could also understand how that child might also feel about me. Wouldn't I want forgiveness for my actions too if it was offered? Yes, I would. With all my heart.

The True Truth set us both free. I was never abandoned; I was always loved. My mother showed me love but I couldn't recognize it from my vantage point. Clearing out those lies has opened up more Vested Truths for me:

➤ I am important.

➤ I was always loved.

➤ I am worthy of protection.

➤ I am worthy of happiness.

➤ I am worthy of love.

➤ My mother loves me unconditionally.

I have learned about both my lies and my worth as well as my Vested Truths in so many different ways over my lifetime. But the discovery of none of these truths or untruths originated within me. They have always come from logic, education, interactions, observances, other people's words and actions, investigation using the Five V's, prayer, meditation, forgiveness, self-forgiveness, open-mindedness and any other form of evidence I may decide to use.

Some of the things I was invested in as being the Truth have been healed and turned in to an unshakable Vested Truth.

If you are still confused at all about what constitutes whether you are "Vested" or not, let me leave you with this:

When I used to be a singer, I had a rumor going around the internet about me. The rumor was that I was really a 6-foot-tall man in drag. They said I may look like a woman, but I was really a man. When I read this to myself, I laughed so hard I nearly cried. I read it to my friends, and we all laughed and laughed at the hilarity of it, because truth be told, I am 5 feet tall for starters, and secondly, I was born a woman and I have given birth to 3 beautiful children. If I were a man, I would not have been able to do this.

I am 100% VESTED in the fact that I am a woman. I am also 100% VESTED in the fact that I am only 5 feet tall. No matter what anyone were to say to try and convince me of something different, I am fully Vested in those truths. Even if those internet people were 100% convinced that I was not 5 feet tall or female, it still wouldn't shake the True Truth inside. No matter how much those people believed what they were saying, anyone who knows me would laugh at the ridiculousness of those words. I AM A 5-FOOT-TALL LITTLE WOMAN. In those truths I am VESTED, and those truths cannot be changed by anyone. Vested = Unchangeable. Vested = The True Truth. Vested = Authenticity.

What are some simple truths you are Vested in? Go ahead, start small and write them down. Start with the obvious. What is your eye color? How tall are you? What is your sexual orientation? Are you male, female, trans? Write down the "unshakable truths" you have inside. The ones that cannot be changed by anyone. Even as simple as the fact that you are "human." These are the VESTED truths you are already aware of.

Use the Five V's to do your own investigation in to your life and start sifting through the things you are only "invested" in as truths. False truths given to you by others which you feel may not be serving your Greater Purpose. These "false truths" are usually things like, "I am worthless", "I am annoying", "no one wants to be around me", "I am unworthy of love", "success is reserved for the lucky", etc.

Hopefully I have sparked some inspiration for healing within you which will, in turn, open the door of healing for many others in your life as well.

When we are truly Vested - truly Vulnerable and using the Five V's to align our lives, we start to allow for other people around us to do the same. As more and more people are able to return to their Authentic Selves, the world heals a little more. Less Victimization happens and less Villains are created.

I thank you for taking the time to read THE FIVE Vs and hope to see you someday in the future at a live event or just pop by and say hello online.

"I wish for you Vestedness and a life full of Joy, Adventure and Love in Abundance"

9

THE FIVE V'S – PRACTICAL APPLICATION

In Coaching people through the process of using the Five V's in their daily lives, it is always my goal to uncover, discover and discard any and all false truths to get through to the freedom of being in the Vested and True Truth. The YOU that you were born to be. The YOU before all of the extra beliefs and judgments were thrown at you indiscriminately and adopted by you whether consciously or unconsciously. This is sometimes a very quick shift in my clients and students inner dialogue. But first there is some really honest work to be done and open mindedness is of paramount importance while doing this work.

I begin with having them take a few days and write down EVERY place they can remember being a Victim to someone else's actions, thoughts, teachings, etc. It doesn't matter how minimal they think it is. I tell them to write it down anyway. For some people it is hard to admit they were a Victim because it is not in their nature to do so. These are people who usually think they are at fault for everything that happens around them. Some have low self-esteem, some feel bad blaming someone they love for their problems. But I remind them, we are on an uncovering mission here. We are not labeling anyone as a "bad person", but more seeing where there may have been another outcome to a situation. For example, I have many clients who think that there has to be a "good guy" and a "bad guy" to any situation where the word Victim shows up. I gently remind my clients that when we look at a situation from the vantage point of everyone involved, we will see a different view of the situation as a whole. For example, if 10 people were standing placed evenly around a building, everyone looking at the building from their view- and the building were to catch fire, each would describe what they were seeing from where they are standing. None of the stories would be exactly the same, but they would all be accurate according to their position.

The same goes for the vantage point of everyone involved in a Victim situation. But the vantage point would be based on their own feelings and dialogue inside of themselves. So, in acknowledging a situation where you are either Victimized or imagine you have been victimized, it is all based on how you feel in the situation. If you imagine someone is a scary or unsafe person when they are not – it doesn't change the Visceral feeling of fear you will have when you see that person. You will shift the way you act when that person is around because of YOUR view, not theirs. I'll give an example.

I lived in a neighborhood once that was full of very "well to do" people. I had worked hard to be able to live in this neighborhood and afford the lease for this home. I was so excited to move in and relax beside my pool during the day, and take walks in a safe and quiet neighborhood. On the day I moved in, I could see the reaction of the neighbors as they watched me and my husband and all our tattoos moving our things in. I had a family of 6 living next door who didn't seem very happy with our presence and the president of the HOA to the other side. They had told me how all the neighbors had been there for decades living next door to each other and were "hoping that a family would have moved into our place." I laughed and told them playfully that they were stuck with me. But not to worry because I was many years sober and the worst thing they would have to deal with would be my Sunday morning meditation group or other sober people coming to visit. They would hear no loud parties and although we looked rambunctious, we would be the best neighbors they could ask for. Telling them I was sober caused a rumor to flow around the neighborhood that I would be inviting "alcoholics" into their neighborhood. Cue the metaphorical pitchforks and torches.

The neighbors never really recovered from the way I looked or the neighbor who spread around the rumor that I was inviting a lower-class type of person into their safe space. They were unwelcoming and even cruel in their actions. They accused me and my guests of things that were both unbelievably outrageous and untrue. Citing that I had visitors in and out all day long and that they believed I was selling drugs. A simple joking and bantering between my husband and his friends were reported as "escalated arguments," even though they were laughing and smiling as they spoke to each other. It was wildly unbelievable, the things our house was reported for. A GQ Magazine delivered in our driveway was reported as "piles of trash" on the street. They tried everything they could to paint me and my husband as "undesirable" to be in their neighborhood. When I would walk around the neighborhood, they would drive their cars down the street and stop the car to watch me walk until I returned to our home. Then report me for walking near their home. There was a whole HOA board hearing on the matter as well. It was very sad. You see, they had a "story" of the truth in their mind about how "tattooed or sober people" were. But this story was not true, and no amount of talking to them, or trying to connect with them helped. I felt like a Victim and wanted to be a Villain. They felt like a Victim and acted out as a Villain. There was no true "bad guy" or "good guy", only people looking at a situation from their own vantage point and judging it based on the things they had been taught by society, parents, etc. The only place to go would be Vulnerable and Vested. I remained open and nice to the neighbors and had to remain Vested in the fact that my tattoos didn't disqualify me from living in that neighborhood. No matter how they felt.

That situation was a gift that I could use to find out what MY True Truths were about myself. I may not have felt like I wanted to call myself a Victim in that situation, but a "normal person of sound mind" could possibly feel like a Victim in my place. So, I did the work on it. I teach the dangers of falling into a Victim mindset. But I had to get down to the true truth and admit I didn't like the way it felt being in that situation. Cue the flashlight shining on some residual Victim beliefs lingering inside my body.

I was able to Viscerally connect to the feelings inside. I got to ask myself what was creating this feeling. Where was I the imagining or labeling myself a Victim? Once I could find that feeling, or thought, I could work on the core beliefs about myself which were still not Vested. THAT was where the healing was still needing to be done. In the Victim role, I could not move out of the Visceral feeling of stuck and afraid. I also gained some empathy for my neighbors in the simple fact that they were also afraid and feeling like Victims of a "scary" new neighbor whom they didn't understand yet. They don't have the gift of doing this work, so they did the next thing that a scared "Victim" quite often does, and they took on the role of a Villain to protect themselves (or so they imagined). I don't fault them for this, I believe that was their "best" at the time.

If you have situations where you could imagine yourself playing either of these roles above, don't fret. We all have these moments. We would hardly be human if we didn't. It's moments like these with which we have choice.

If we "choose" to remain in a Victim role when we are feeling like one, we automatically slip into the role of our own Villain. How you ask?

It's simple. If our parents left us standing in the rain as a child, shame on them. But if we are still standing in the rain as an adult complaining or blaming our parents for leaving us there, shame on us.

Remember, being a Victim or a Villain is going against your true nature. It isn't your True Truth. There is no solution offered in those roles. So, get out, now.

Back to our work. Once a client writes down all of their "Victim" moments in their life. I ask them next to explain where they are a Villain in their life. We approach this a number of ways.

First. A lot of time we can look at all of the Victim roles they have already written down, and I will talk through it with them – asking them, since you are no longer presently in that Victim situation and you are currently in the NOW, in what way are you choosing to stay in the mindset of a Victim? Do you continually feel the feelings these situations have left you with? Do you revisit this moment in your head and replay the scenario again and again? Do you say something different in your mind? Do you imagine yourself winning? Retaliating? Do you find some way to regain your personal power when you imagine this moment again? Do you talk about it to others and try to find someone to affirm you were a Victim? Stop! You have now become your own Villain! You no longer need the players in this situation to take your power, because you are now giving it away yourself.

Simply accept that you deserved better. You did. Or maybe you needed that situation to find your power and change the things you choose to allow into your current life. Find the gift in the tragedy. What did you learn from it? Where can you heal the way YOU see YOU from it? Who can you help with your newfound wisdom? What lie did this situation plant in you about your personal worth? Is it the True Truth?

I ask my clients if they can see how we can get caught in the Victim / Villain cycle forever. There is no true power in that cycle. It is an insanity that seems to go on and on. We will find ourselves choosing similar situations to work through the feelings with by finding all new players and scenarios. I have a simpler way for you to break the Victim / Villain cycle. Acknowledge, honor your pain and then find the True Truth about you.

I point out to my students that the Visceral awareness is how we know whether we are in Victim, Villain or Vested. When feeling fear or insecurity, we have a Visceral disturbance which makes it clear that we are in Victim or Villain. Once we find the True Truth and become Vested in who we are, what we believe and what we deserve, our Visceral will calm down and we will feel empowered. Until then, keep digging.

The 4th V, Vulnerable is the power behind the machine. Our Villain will want to keep us angry or keep us in the Victim role, it thinks it's safer when others are to blame for our misfortunes. But we cannot afford to let our Villain role win. When we can get truly Vulnerable with ourselves and allow ourselves to feel the pain, love ourselves in spite of our errors and accept ourselves as simply human – we can truly heal.

Blame and shame need to leave our world for us to be free of the Victim / Villain trap. Yes, it is an emotional trap. When we blame others or ourselves, or adopt a shame that doesn't let up, we are trapped. This is not to say that we shouldn't make right the situations where we have harmed another or ourselves, I definitely recommend this to everyone if it is safe to do so. Making right the things we have made wrong clears up our spiritual scoreboard per se. It frees us from the past and allows for a new direction to the future. But first we must find our Vested Truth. The True Truth. This is done with my clients on a personal level. Once we find what we imagine or instinctively know should be the Vested True Truth about ourselves. We then ask ourselves some questions.

Does this Vested Truth feel Viscerally true?

Is this Vested Truth something every innocent child has a right to?

Does this Vested Truth empower us and others?

Would the world be better with you in it if this was your Vested True Truth?

Is the love inside restored?

As I said before, this is a coaching style that I use with my clients in person. I know I may be unable to go through the work with every person who would benefit from it. But hopefully some of this book can help you navigate through these things by yourself. If you are truly looking for empowerment, I hope I have made sense to you, the reader.

Now I will leave you with one of my favorite assignments I give to my clients. The Forgiveness Prayer.

10 - FORGIVENESS WORK

It may become evident after reading this book that one of the most important people you must learn to forgive is yourself. I am not going to write a great deal in this section -However, I will share with you a little piece of self-forgiveness work that I often choose to give to new students and clients before they can begin to make changes in their lives.

The Forgiveness Script

You can begin using Forgiveness to diffuse your blocks to growth at any time. You need only decide that you are open to The True Truth.

Once a client experiences the need for change, they often find themselves unable to merge the knowledge they have learned and know to be true in their Head Brain, with what they know be true in their other Two Brains (Heart and Gut). When we are faced with such a challenge, I give my students an assignment of "Forgiveness Work" so they can begin moving forward.

Here is a simple thing you can do to help with forgiveness of self. It was given to me by my friend,

Heather.

Take a piece of paper and a pen and write the following down:

"YOUR NAME",

I LOVE YOU AND I FORGIVE YOU FOR ALL PAST, "PERCEIVED" WRONGS. THE TRUTH IS, YOU WERE DOING THE BEST YOU COULD AT THE TIME...

AND IF YOU COULD HAVE DONE BETTER, YOU WOULD HAVE. I FORGIVE YOU; I LOVE YOU AND I SET YOU FREE.

Paste this on a mirror and LOOK YOURSELF IN THE EYES while you repeat this to yourself 10x per day.

Most people who begin this forgiveness work will experience a strong, Visceral Reaction. Let your feelings come without judgment.

We've had enough judgment for one lifetime already. It's time for some different thinking.

For most who do this exercise, they report that they have a major shift almost immediately.

Remember, there are no adults standing over you and demanding you pay for your wrongs anymore (if there are, read the book again).

Now, the only authority you need to convince and confirm to you that you deserve happiness is yourself.

Use this Forgiveness work to help heal your mind. You deserve to be healed and happy. You have a Divine Right to all the things you were born with.

11

CLIENT & PEER TESTIMONIALS

One of my great honors this year was sharing the stage with my sister Franki. She is an inspiring and powerful woman. She let me read her book the Five V's and it's inspiring and powerful. She shares her teachings with anyone who is ready to begin a journey that is ready to let go of whatever doesn't serve them anymore. She will listen, guide and support with such an open heart. When you are ready, she will be there!!!

Don Jose Ruiz
Author of The Wisdom of The Shamans
Co-Author of "The Fifth Agreement"

I've had the honor of working alongside Franki as a group facilitator at the Infinite Possibilities Train the Trainer event (2018) with Mike Dooley as well as hiring her to speak at that event. As the director of training, I worked closely with her and observed her gift for seeing others and igniting their potential. As a speaker, she held and moved the room with the power of her story, her illuminating wisdom and magnetism. Her heart and passion to empower others is palpable in every conversation and speech. She's an inspiring teacher, speaker and facilitator and we were blessed to have her talent and integrity grace our event.

Regena Schwarz Garrepy
Creatrix at Regena Garrepy, LLC
IP Director of Training / Mike Dooley

I have had the privilege of working closely with Franki for over 5 years and when asked if I would provide a few words about her coaching style and teaching method — I didn't even think twice. I am of the belief system that people are capable of achieving anything they want with hard work, dedication and practice at their craft. With that being said I also believe that people deep down in their core, due to their circumstance, their upbringing, their skillset and their soul have the perfect combination of traits to be the very best at something should they ever be lucky enough to find what that is. Franki found hers. Prior to working with Franki, I wasn't a believer. I wasn't a believer in the 5 V's, of her coaching or to be brutally honest, I wasn't a believer in myself. It wasn't until I sat down with her for the first time that I realized how wrong I truly was. She has mastered her craft and I truly believe was put on this earth to fill the role of a teacher and instructor of self-love. I'd say my life has completely changed, but that would sound so cliché and unauthentic. But the facts are these; after doing some coaching with Franki, the way that I view life has changed, the way that I view what I am capable of has changed and the way that I view myself has drastically changed and for that, I'll always be indebted to Franki.

Corey Richman
Vice President
Vinea Consulting, LLC

The last time I saw Franki speak on stage she shared her heart and soul. She inspires everyone with her stories and insights and of course the audience gave her a standing ovation. If you have not met Franki yet, your time is now. Get ready to discover your personal power and allow her to guide you into your deepest truth so you can activate your full potential! BUYEAH!

Andy Dooley
Author, Coach, Motivator

There are no words in modern language to describe this woman. She has completely changed my life from damaged and blindly walking through this world, to healing and finding my greatness. I mean, I named my daughter after the woman!!! As a 6'4 250lb man raised in a military family, Ive been very good at keeping people out ... Franki is the only person that not only was brave enough to push me but wise enough to find the real me. Pure Love.

Jason Lawson
Owner & Founder
Personal Rehabilitative Solutions

Franki is a beautiful, powerful, loving. dynamic teacher. She has an intuitive strength that cuts through old belief patterns that have been so normalized that they have become invisible. She is fire when I've needed a wake-up call and is calm, cool, loving and nurturing when that has been much needed. There are few people in whom I trust to let go, allow them to see beneath the surface, and guide me into a higher understanding of my Self, my place in this Universe, and my unacknowledged potential. Franki is one of them. I would recommend Franki to anyone, not because she will coax you and make your spiritual 'boo boo's' feel better, but because she truly loves her clients too much to give them anything other than what they need.

Max Rennie
Owner & CEO
Maxwell's Mystic Matches

Let me just start by saying that prior to doing work with Franki and implementing what I've learned from the Five V's, my life was stuck in a vicious cycle of chronic self-victimization. I was constantly flooded with feelings of guilt & shame for mistakes I made in my life. I always had my fingers pointed, never truly taking responsibility for my actions. Everything was everyone else's fault and I was sure of it.

This mindset, along with a combination of other things, eventually lead me down the dark & twisted path of addiction. After a while, I had enough and embarked on my journey of recovery. I found the solution I needed to help me stay on the straight & narrow. However, the same feelings of guilt & shame came creeping back in.

A friend recommended I attend a coaching class from Franki, and boy do I have **ZERO** regrets. I could go into great detail about how this inspiring, loving woman has helped me. I'll keep it concise though. Franki introduced me to her Five V's and coached me along the way to a new path of freedom. She showed me how not only was I a professional VICTIM, but how I had also been the MAIN VILLAIN in my story. This was a new concept for me. The process that Franki lays out in the Five V's was not always an easy one for me. BUT, the level of freedom and peace I've gotten from it is second to none. I was able to transform my pain from my mistakes - from paralyzing guilt & shame into a tool for helping others. I am truly comfortable and happy with who I am today. These are just some of the gifts I've received from the Five V's. The rest you'll have to discover for yourself.

Hayden Moser
Aspiring Life Coach

From personal experience, when I started coaching with Franki I was suicidal, hopeless and completely defeated. I was a chronic relapser, I've been doing the same thing over and over again for 4 years. I was desperate. This

experience was the most impactful, life changing experience. I received a gift that is internally priceless. The gift to accept myself, to be content in self, learn to love myself first, find my internal truth, find my voice. I've learned to stand up for myself and recovery, become a respectful and respected woman, set healthy boundaries, develop a strong support network, become empowered, kept accountable, work a solid 12 Step program, to get uncomfortable because that's where the growth happens. I've learned to just be. I've learned how to relax and developed coping skills that work with my individuality. Codependency recovery, I've learned the power of my thoughts and how to rewire/ change my thinking, I've learned the abundance of being who I truly am, learned how to have healthy relationships, I've learned value of myself and others, I've learned how to release the past, I've learned to open up, I learned how to not allow my emotions to control me and my life, I've learned how to do life again (get a job, have healthy relationships with friends and family, have a healthy relationship with a significant other, self-care, boundary setting, to make the most out of what I have, to practice gratitude, balance, to reach out to my support network whom my life coach guided me too, stress managing etc...) and most of all I learned what I thought I lost... to be happy again. If it wasn't for this incredibly, beautiful enlightened woman opening up her heart to me, I would not be here today.
This woman saved my life.

Katie Morrow
Dog Lover / Stay at home Mom

Working with Franki has been nothing short of a miracle. When I met her, I was scared, defeated, confused and completely lost. What I admire about Franki's work the most is that she doesn't hold my hand and force me to drink from the water. She has taught me how to connect to the enchanted waters in my heart space through self-love. Through being aware of my thought process. Franki demonstrates through action what this work does and gives me permission to be my best self and follow suit. Connecting with the 5 V's has liberated me in a way words cannot possibly describe. Having a map of my ongoing patterns has allowed for me to break free. But what do I do with that freedom? Within the 5 V's I've been given that path to freedom. Mapping out my patterns with Victim and Villain has made me aware of the situations I've been continuously putting myself in unconsciously. Running around in circles and confused as to how I even got here. Moving into the visceral portion I can identify that all of this is a lie. I am not a victim nor am I a villain. I have to be truly vulnerable with myself and others to identify when I'm moving into these patterns. Lastly comes vested. With all this new information I who am I now? What kind of woman do I want to be? Franki helped me decipher how I want to conduct myself in this world. What do I want to invest in? What matters to me? In place of all these things who do I want to be? Well, through these V's I've discovered I'm Vested in empowerment. I'm Vested in peace. I'm Vested in connecting to humanity. I'm Vested in creativity. I'm Vested in freedom. I'm Vested in my journey as a woman moving back into her soul. I'm Vested in this work. I'm so grateful for Franki and all of her dedication to setting her fellows truly free through loving awareness.

With Love,
Sarah Chasteen
Spiritual Teacher / Breath Works Instructor

Hi, my name is Costas Vasilakis. I am a 28 year-old man originally from Connecticut. I originally moved out to California in search of sobriety and a stable/supportive recovery community. Having had recently come off of a homeless episode of daily meth and heroin use, I was in desperate need of some help and support which I found immediately found in the recovery community of OC California.

Within that community I met Franki. Throughout our brief interactions, I noticed that she was a bit different. Different in the sense that her daily interactions were truly genuine as well as her all around positive vibe and aura. Shortly after these initial interactions, she came up to me one night and invited me to her spirituality-based meetings she held at her home stating "I think you would be perfect for these meetings". Initially I was nervous to attend but having been directed to explore personal growth by the people who have walked the road of sobriety before me, I accepted the invite. I can honestly say that the recovery community in OC has saved my life however, NOTHING has transformed my life and perception/approach to life in the way that The Five V's and Franki's Coaching Group which she calls "The Tribe of Elephants" has.

The name derives from the simple fact that elephants by nature will surround sick or injured members of the pact to protect them and ensure safety and recovery from said injury or illness. This is first and foremost exactly what I found here. With that group environment being established, Franki has successfully been able to transform the lives of myself and many others with The Five V's and other Spiritual concepts she coaches others in.

Franki has taught me many things such as the law of attraction and manifestation. Naturally being slightly skeptical to these concepts and practices, I was quickly convinced otherwise by Frankis ability to lead by example. This quickly allowed me to buy in to the truth. Through this group, I have found a family and through this group I have found a new and genuine excitement for life. First and foremost, she has taught me to believe that my dreams are already a reality and that my biggest obstacle is my confidence and belief in their manifestation. She has taught me how to remove agreements and conditioning I have acquired throughout my life and replace them with agreements that serve my greater purpose. She has taught me how to show up for other and more importantly, how to show up for myself.

One thing I have found extremely beneficial from her method of coaching and teaching is not only her educational knowledge, but her exercises and "challenges" she gives us. Throughout these exercises and challenges I have witnessed in my own life as well as others, financial growth after financial growth. Relationship growth after relationship growth. Personal growth after personal growth and a countless amount of amazing adventures in throughout. "Why not you?!" she replies when I question my dreams and aspirations. "Because I love you is why I am going to tell you the truth right now. Not just what you want to hear" she says when my perception is standing in the way of my greater/higher self. She always challenges us with one goal and intention in mind, to bring out who we really are at the core of everything and allow us to unleash our greatest form of self. Our truest form of self. I am without a doubt convinced today that Franki was supposed to enter my life when she did, and I feel truly blessed and grateful that she did and that I have been gifted this opportunity for growth and personal exploration.

To anyone who is hesitant or questioning whether or not they should explore the concepts and practices I have learned from Franki and the Tribe of elephants, I urge you to jump in with an open mind. It is truly transformative in the greatest of ways and to anyone who has the opportunity to work directly with Franki, I strongly urge you to take that opportunity. Between my relationship with her as well as her husband Jenson who has mentored me through some of the most confusing as well as exciting times of my life, I have found not only a home, but a complete change and shift in perception of my approach to life. This has truly allowed me to "live" in the truest sense of the word and for that Franki, I say "Thank you".

Costas Vasilakis

ABOUT THE AUTHOR

Franki Olinger is a retired musician and actress who found her true happiness as a teacher of Spirituality, Empowerment, the Law of Attraction and Love. Franki took a leap of faith and retired from chasing her dreams to be a "rock star" or a famous "actress" because deep inside she knew her calling was in helping others. Even though Franki traveled the world playing music, which she loved. She also did forms of public speaking. The satisfaction from getting off the stage of a speaking event and connecting with those who were there to listen was beyond fulfilling. Franki has helped thousands of people over the past few decades to heal and connect with their True Truth and Vested selves through meditation, workshops, retreats and in person coaching. Franki empowers her clients to dream and create a better world for themselves & everyone they encounter. Franki lives in South Orange County, California with her husband Jenson.

Franki says *"I didn't set out to be a spiritual teacher - but somehow over the years, I found myself surrounded with people who wanted more for their lives than what they currently thought was possible. I had a rough childhood - abuse and even breaking up with a man who shot himself in front of me that same night. I didn't think I would ever find happiness... not only did I find it - I also, in the process became a person who is pretty darned great at helping others to find it as well. I love my life, I love humans... I love what I do!"* Franki Olinger

Made in the USA
Columbia, SC
07 May 2020

93570239R00146